WILLIAM CARLOS WILLIAMS

THE MAKERS OF MODERN LITERATURE SERIES

William Carlos Williams

BY VIVIENNE KOCH

THE MAKERS OF MODERN LITERATURE

New Directions Books - Norfolk, Connecticut

MANUFACTURED IN THE UNITED STATES
BY THE VAIL-BALLOU PRESS, INC.

*New Directions Books Are Published by
James Laughlin*

NEW YORK OFFICE—333 SIXTH AVENUE

TO

MY FATHER

LEGEND

For purposes of space-saving, throughout the book the author refers to Dr. Williams' *Collected Poems* volume as *CP*, to the *Complete Collected Poems* as *CCP*, to manuscript works in the Lockwood Memorial Library of the University of Buffalo as the U.B. Collection, and to all other manuscripts owned by Dr. Williams to which the author has had access as follows: MS I (Prose 1914–1929); MS II (Five Early Essays); MS III ("Paris— Early Marriage"); MS IV (Letters from Williams' mother, their joint translation of *The Dog and the Fever*, notes and sketches).

C O N T E N T S

WILLIAM CARLOS WILLIAMS

Photograph by Charles Sheeler
(1926)

P R E F A C E

THE CRITIC WHO ATTEMPTS A FULL-LENGTH CRITICAL ESTI-
mate of a living writer exposes himself to charges of
partiality if his conclusions are favorable, or, if his conclusions are unfavorable, to those of prejudice. In either
case, he is exposed to the real possibility that he may be
too close to his subject, a situation which may result in
a distortion of perspective. But this is not nearly so dangerous to either critic or subject as some would have it.
Criticism is not written as a signature for eternity but as
a discipline in extending the limits of that receptivity
with which the reader approaches the work criticized.
Thus, the critic's first job is to develop the reader's ear
so that it responds to the artist's personal voice and
idiom.

This book was written without Dr. Williams' knowledge, although I have often talked with him about his
work and have read various unpublished manuscripts in
his possession.

I am indebted to Mr. James Laughlin both for the original suggestion for this study, and for the emended galley proofs of *Paterson Book 1* which he has given me. As Dr. Williams' chief publisher, he is also to be thanked for permission to quote from the various works.

I am thankful to Norman Macleod for his suggestions at the planning stage of this book.

I wish to thank Mrs. Ivah Sweeney, Assistant to the Director of the Lockwood Memorial Library of the University of Buffalo, for her help in the use of the Williams MS Collection which I have found of invaluable service.

I should explain that my liberal paraphrase of some of Williams' unpublished work as well as of some of the earlier published work, now out of print, has been necessary because I could not refer the reader to an available text.

Vivienne Koch

I

THE POEMS

IT IS IN POETRY THAT WILLIAMS' ACHIEVEMENT PROMISES
to be most enduring. There are some good poets whose
destiny appears as rigidly determined as a formula in
calculus. Marianne Moore is such a poet. She is of Williams' generation and has been exposed to the same literary currents. But reading her last work in *Nevertheless*
(1944) and admiring the lathelike precision of its wit, one
finds little that one might not have predicted from *Observations* (1924). This is not to deny Miss Moore her
development but merely to point to its inevitability. Examining Dr. Williams' poetry, we proceed, as perhaps the
poet himself did, by a series of shocks. Looking at a
recent poem, "The Pink Church," a rich hymn of avowal,
one remembers the Luther-inspired sonnet composed in
1909 when Williams was a young medical student in
Germany. The gap of almost forty years in composition
is not as great as the distance between the two poems.
Before this sonnet and the first tiny, blue-covered collec-

tion of *Poems,* written between 1906 and 1909 while a student at the University of Pennsylvania along with Ezra Pound and H.D., Williams has written some poetry, mostly acrostics, none of which have been preserved. The following acrostic composed for Hilda Doolittle's birthday book in 1905 has been got up from memory by Dr. Williams:

> Hark Hilda, heptachordian hymns
> Invoke the year's initial ides
> Like liquid lutes low languishings
> Dim dawn defeated dusk derides
> Awake! for at Aurora's advent angel
> anthemnings arise.

The first *Poems* reveal little concerning Williams' future direction. Like Wallace Stevens' collegiate work, they are conventional, correct in sentiment and diction, and the only extraordinary feature is their ordinariness. The titles reflect a range of subject-matter that should have proved acceptable to genteel magazines like *Harpers'* and *The Atlantic Monthly* against whose dictation of standards in American poetry Williams was to fight so militantly a few years later. *Poems* reflects a docile acceptance of the "tradition" of English poetry then operative. For like Ezra Pound and T. S. Eliot, Williams had read the Romantic poets: "Keats with fascination, Shelley without conviction and not thoroughly, Byron (*Don Juan* only) but fascinated" and, I suspect, much of Browning. It was some time, however, before the presence of Browning could be detected in Williams' poetry. Other poets read at this time were Spenser, Chaucer, Marlowe, Palgrave's *Golden Treasury,* all the plays of Synge, and

2

THE POEMS

"More outstanding than any other reading for me were the plays of Shakespeare . . ."

Yet, under the conventional surface of the Luther sonnet, written a short while later, after a visit to the Wartburg, one senses a restlessness in the curious rime-scheme (*abba, cbbc, acca*), in the omission of the final couplet, and in the ingenious internal repetition of the beat of the bird's song. The sonnet, as printed here, has been reconstructed from memory by Dr. Williams:

> Alone today I mounted that steep hill
> On which the Wartburg stands, here Luther dwelt
> A year through at his labors, here he spelt
> The German Bible out by God's goodwill.
>
> The birds piped ti-ti-tuh and as I went
> I thought how Katharin von Borah knelt
> At Grimma, idle she, waiting to melt
> Her surpliced heart in folds less straitly meant.
>
> As now, it was March then, lo! he'll fulfill
> Today his mighty task, sing for content
> Ye birds, pipe now! for now 'tis love's wing bent
> Work sleeps, love wakes, sing! and the glad air thrill.

Felicitous as are a few of the phrases for their plainness of diction ("he spelt the German Bible out by God's goodwill," "Her surpliced heart in folds less straitly meant"), the sonnet retains enough stock vocabulary to have made it fall lightly upon refined academic ears in 1909, although the faulty opening line of the third quatrain and the banal end-rimes of "fill" and "thrill" might have offended the purist. It is interesting that Williams considers this sonnet a link between the *Poems* and the first items in the *CP*.

· · · ·

3

By the time Dr. Williams' first commercially published collection came out in England in 1913 under the imprimatur of Elkin Matthews, through the mediation of Ezra Pound, the Wartburg poem and the effete tradition it reflected had receded into the limbo of early trials. Williams was now oriented differently. He was again responding to a tradition, but now to the more exotic one of the Provençal lyric which Ezra Pound had so vigorously employed in the songs and translations in *A Lume Spento* (1908), *Personae* (1908), *Exultations* (1909), *Canzoni* (1911), and *Ripostes* (1913). As Harriet Monroe notes in *A Poet's Life:* "Dr. Williams seemed to be an auxiliary rather than a disciple of his militant friend in London." Still, there are some lyrics in *The Tempers* which are transparently, even brilliantly Poundian—the Pound of Cavalcanti and Arnaut Daniel, the Pound of those moving appreciations, "Altaforte," and "A Virginal." The grace with which Williams caught Pound's backward-glancing lyricism is displayed in the lovely "Homage":

> Elvira, by love's grace
> There goeth before you
> A clear radiance
> Which maketh all vain souls
> Candles when noon is.
>
> The loud clangour of pretenders
> Melteth before you
> Like the roll of carts passing,
> But come silently
> And homage is given.
>
> Now the little by-path
> Which leadeth to love

> Is again joyful with its many;
> And the great highway
> From love
> Is without passers.

Several of the poems in *The Tempers* had had the benefit of Miss Monroe's grave corrections, for she had printed them in her recently established magazine, *Poetry*. Still, it is amusing to note how limited were even her "advanced" tastes when we find her suggesting to the young poet-physician that "Peace on Earth" should have "a more explanatory title" and that "Proof of Immortality" lacks an iambic syllable in the fourth and sixth lines. But Williams was not one to take this careful advice without some lively inquiry. Miss Monroe, looking back thirty years, wrote: "Williams' prompt answer to my exceptions gave me a jolt into free spaces. I still find his letter suggestive enough to be quoted for the benefit of editors." In it Williams questioned the propriety of the functions Miss Monroe had assigned to poet and editor:

The poet comes forth assailing the trite and the established, while the editor is to shear off all roughness and extravagance . . . Now life is above all things at any moment subversive of life as it was the moment before—always new, irregular. Verse to be alive must have infused into it something of the same tincture of disestablishment, something in the nature of an impalpable revolution . . .
Surely if Yeats teaches anything that can be learnt—that is, anything that would not be copying to take to oneself—he teaches what can be done with the three syllable foot every time but once or twice in the entire poem. Witness "The Mountain Tomb" in your own *Poetry* . . .

Miss Monroe had opened the pages of *Poetry* to a discussion of Imagism as early as November 1912. During this period, as well, Pound and Williams were in close correspondence. One would therefore expect a reflection of the practice recommended by the Imagists in the poems of *The Tempers*. To the contrary, they suggest a considerable range of formal influences. In "Lullaby" a conventional Georgian song structure is cleverly manipulated, while "Immortal" is a bright usage of the Classical epigram. "Contemporaria," an expansion of the Japanese *hokku*, does indirectly reflect the Imagist's interest in Oriental poetry which had been stimulated by Pound. "Postlude," "Mezzo-Forte," and "First Praise" all have a conversational, Poundian flavor although the similarity probably derives from the common obligation of both poets to Browning. "An After Song" dramatizes the struggle then raging in the young poet's mind: classical subjects break in upon "modern twilight" and seem "strange." In this early book, it is the poems of love which are most intensely felt and most simply stated. They are closest to the tone of Williams' later work.

. . . .

By the time Williams' new poems (see "Transitional" in *CCP*) appeared in various magazines during 1915 he had been fully exposed to the rather carefully contrived pyrotechnics of the Imagist movement. Ezra Pound's first Imagist anthology came out in New York in February 1914, under the title, *Des Imagistes*. Williams was in the new anthology which, as Richard Aldington makes clear in *Life for Life's Sake*, had little programmatic direction and merely grew out of Pound's suggestion that he, Aldington, and the latter's wife, H.D., publish a joint collection of their poems. Ford Madox Ford, for example, was a well-established author and they liked his poems, "although there was nothing very imagistic about them . . . Joyce and Carlos Williams were also most acceptable." The edition, according to Mr. Aldington, immediately sold out and became a *succés de scandale*. "Columnists parodied the poems or reproduced them (without payment) accompanied by derisive remarks."

Meanwhile, Williams had continued publishing in *Poetry*, as well as in Alfred Kreymborg's *The Glebe*, Wyndham Lewis' *Blast* and in various other of the impressive number of advance guard reviews which were springing up on both sides of the Atlantic. This period marked the height of the free-verse controversy which derived from the precepts of Imagism. Williams, as we shall see, has since made some illuminating comments on the nature of his own "Imagism." While the label sticks, it is meaningful now only as a historical setting for Williams' early verse, rather than as a description of it.

The most salutary effect of Imagism to be found in the "Transitional" group is in the crisp "free-verse" line which begins to appear. But, as the letter written to Miss Monroe in 1912 indicates, Williams had begun to think about the problem of measure even before the publication of Ezra Pound's Imagist manifesto in the pages of *Poetry* in March 1913. While the "issue" of *vers libre* would seem now to be dead, a serious critic like Yvor Winters, once a *vers librist* himself, was able ten years ago to exhume the corpse in *Primitivism and Decadence* with sufficient cunning to make the problem seem temporarily alive. Without

7

seeking to repeat the performance, or to reopen wounds which history has healed, a brief discussion of the matter is in order.

Williams has, in a remarkably single-minded way, continued the interest in measure of which we see evidence in the letter to Miss Monroe. What he has worked out is not a "new verse line," for Winters' notion of "the line" would appear as false to him as the notion of a received lyric "form," but rather a range of verse measures that are flexibly dependent on what they seek to do with the materials they organize. In 1912 Pound published a Prolegomena in the English *Poetry Review* in which he said with his customary point: *"Rhythm*—I believe in an 'Absolute rhythm,' a rhythm that is, in poetry which corresponds exactly to an emotion or shade of emotion to be expressed . . ."* Still only five years later in *A Retrospect* he was to say, qualifying his earlier view, but adding to the confusion, that

the desire for *vers libre* is due to the sense of quantity reasserting itself after years of starvation, but I doubt if we can take over, for English, the rules of quantity laid down for Greek and Latin . . . I think one should write *vers libre* only when one "must" that is to say, only when the "thing" builds up a rhythm more beautiful than that of set metres, or more real, more a part of the emotion of the "thing" . . . than the measure of regular accentual verse; a rhythm which discontents one with set iambic or set anapaestic.

It must certainly have come as news to the *vers librists* that they were writing a kind of quantitative measure. And if an observation of the *"rules"* of quantity defined the practice of these poets one wonders where the "libre" came in. I know of no poems classifiable as Imagist which could be scanned or read even quasi-quantitatively, let alone by the principles of classical quantitative prosody. Certainly neither Williams, Pound himself, nor any of his group have, to my knowledge, written a poem even remotely conforming to quantitative laws.

The possibility of such writing is, by the way, an interesting and as yet open question, for while it is clear that classical quantity cannot be introduced into English without a ridiculous falsification of both the prosody and the English, at the same time experimental studies in recent years have demonstrated a fairly reliable correspondence between quantity and accent in *spoken* English. That is to say, a long syllable tends to correspond to a heavy accent and a short syllable to a light accent. Roughly, long syllables (accented) tend to be twice as long as short syllables (unaccented) so that—in theory at least —it might be possible to work out a crudely quantitative system for English. The point of such a discipline would, it seems to me, be almost entirely lost precisely because of the rough identity of quantitative and accentual norms in English, so that the tug of the accentual pattern would eventually either iron out the bias of the quantitative arrangement or run a parallel course to it.

Pound, in a later recantation, recognized some other principle beside "quantity" as operative in his own "free verse" practice:

". . . there is *vers libre* with accent heavily marked as a drum beat (as par example my 'Dance Figure') and on the other hand . . . I do not think one can use to any advantage rhythms much more tenuous and imperceptible than some I have used. I think progress lies rather in an attempt to approximate classical quantitative metres (NOT to copy them) . . ."

9

But as to *what* free verse is we have no testimony either from Pound or anyone else. Pound quotes Eliot approvingly as saying "no *vers* is *libre* for the man who wants to do a good job." And elsewhere Eliot wrote "Vers Libre has not even the excuse of a polemic; it is a battle cry of freedom, and there is no freedom in art." In spite of this legislative talk, Eliot has himself continued on and off to write free verse. One might point to passages in *Four Quartets* which Raymond Preston, in an exegesis which had Mr. Eliot's reading, describes as "free verse."

It is important to understand that in these early poems Williams was investigating the possibilities not of *a* line or *a* measure but of many combinations of unrhymed accentual patterns closer to the cadences of heard speech. This interest is disguised in the conventional mask of the Browning monologue. The rather simple expedient of holding on to the monologue form as a direct vehicle for speech experience, also attracted Pound and at about the same time. But it is instructive to see how differently the two poets assimilated Browning to their own leanings. Compare, for example, the anapaestic cast of Pound's moving soliloquy, "Villanelle: The Psychological Hour," first published in *Blast* in 1914:

> I had over-prepared the event,
> that much was ominous.

with the short, heavily spondaic trimeter and tetrameter line of Williams' wry "Le Médecin Malgré Lui":

> Oh I suppose I should
> wash the walls of my office

        polish the rust from
        my instruments and keep them
        definitely in order
        build shelves in the laboratory
        empty out the old stains
        clean the bottles
        and refill them, buy
        another lens, put
        my journals on edge instead of
        letting them lie flat
        in heaps—then begin
        ten years back and
        gradually
        read them to date
        cataloguing important
        articles for ready reference.
        I suppose I should
        read the new books.
        If to this I added
        a bill at the tailor's
        and at the cleaner's
        grew a decent beard
        and cultivated a look
        of importance—
        Who can tell? I might be
        a credit to my Lady Happiness
        and never think anything
        but a white thought!

The crisp, matter-of-fact diction of "Le Médecin Malgré Lui" and its casual tone of exposition contrive together an insinuating counterpoint to the serious ethical crisis described by the title. The apparent directness of the autobiography saves it from sentimentality.

The fine "Portrait of a Lady" is closer in style and atmosphere to the Provençal lyric tradition which had produced the delicate "Postlude." Pound in 1917 naming "the few beautiful poems that still ring in my head" lists the latter along with Joyce's "I Hear an Army," and Yeats's "The Fire That Stirs About Her When She Stirs." "Portrait of a Lady" adds to its graceful movement the new hint of a robust anti-romantic bias and heightens this element by incorporating the colloquial strain of "Le Médecin Malgré Lui."

> Your thighs are appletrees
> whose blossoms touch the sky.
> Which sky? The sky
> where Watteau hung a lady's
> slipper. Your knees
> are a southern breeze—or
> a guest of snow. Agh! what
> sort of man was Fragonard?
> —as if that answered
> anything. Ah, yes—below
> the knees, since the tune
> drops that way, it is
> one of those white summer days,
> the tall grass of your ankles
> flickers upon the shore—
> Which shore?—
> the sand clings to my lips—
> Which shore?
> Agh, petals maybe. How
> should I know?
> Which shore? Which shore?
> I said petals from an appletree.

The connotations in this still so charming poem occur simultaneously on three levels of experience—art, nature (grass, flowers, trees, as well as the anatomy of the lady herself) and the subjective biography of the poet as he seeks

to relate into some acceptable scheme of "love" the features of the first two. The last eight lines of the poem,
following the descending order of emotion suggested by
the lines "Ah, yes—below the knees, since the tune/drops
that way . . . ," to the willful contradiction of the last
line, "I said petals from an appletree," leave the lover's
attitude toward the lady delicately unresolved in a perilous
universe of whimsical, yet sardonic, ambiguity. The poet
is not only spoofing the lady; he is spoofing himself for his
own "poetical" spoofing.

Looked at as a unit, the poems gathered together in
"Transitional" mark the end of Williams' association with
Imagism. Many years later he was to say when addressing
a group of undergraduates at Dartmouth:

You see, all literary movements are movements, in a large measure,
toward new definition—or at least a definition that seems at the moment necessary. And such a movement in a group will have different
effects in the mind of each man . . .

And in a talk at Harvard in 1941 he put the matter thus:

Imagism, which had a use in focusing the attention upon the importance of concrete imagery in the poem, lost its place finally because as a form it completely lacked structural necessity. The image
served for everything so that the structure, a weaker and weaker free
verse, degenerated finally into a condition very nearly resembling
that of the sonnet.

It is gratifying that Williams does not say "visual" imagery
but "concrete" imagery. The historical vulgarizers of
Imagism customarily identify it with visual data. Ford
Madox Ford summed up the real achievement of the Imagists when he said in his introduction to the *Imagist Anthol-*

ogy of 1930 "Poetry . . . is a matter of rendering, not comment." Ruskin, fifty years earlier, writing on the pathetic fallacy, had said something strikingly like it.

. . . .

As is obvious from Pound's retrospective view of Imagism written in 1917, the "movement," impulse, emphasis had worn itself out long since. Born in 1911, buried and almost forgotten in 1917, Imagism had a short life and not even a merry one. When Williams' next book appeared in 1917, the break with his earlier poetry was cleanly accomplished. *Al Que Quiere!* describes the toughening up process Williams had undergone in the intervening years. Literary polemics, the obfuscating attacks of the professional critics against the Imagists, as well as a new conception of where his materials lay, all contributed to a new tone. Now the strain which Wallace Stevens has somewhat too conveniently termed the "anti-poetic" appears. Concurrently, the increased stress on American subject-matter tends to collaborate with these "anti-poetic" elements.

The epigraph to the original edition of *Al Que Quiere!*, taken from the Latin American playwright, Rafael Arévalo Martínez, illuminates this new emphasis. One sentence is especially significant: *"Había sido un arbusto dismedrado que prolongo sus filamentos hasta encontrar el humus necessario en una tierra nueva. Y como me nutrio!"* It was precisely the discovery of new soil from which he could draw nourishment that Williams celebrated in the poems. That soil was America, America as it could be discovered in Rutherford, on the Passaic, in New Jersey.

THE POEMS

In various creative disciplines, during this decade, a new interest in the American past had been increasing in complexity and vigor, stimulated partly by the war, as well as by Van Wyck Brooks's pioneer attempts to distill the spirit of the American past. From distillation to use-ability had been the direction of Brooks's inquiry. But Williams was not of a temper to be intrigued by the search for a "useable past." Besides his precarious position as a first generation American, the son of an English father and a Puerto Rican mother, living in a small American town in which he was attempting to satisfy the ambivalent demands put upon him by his daily work as a physician and his activity as a writer, Williams had also had the profitable but perhaps unsettling experience of some schooling abroad. At thirteen he and his younger brother, Edward, had been taken by their mother for a year of study in Switzerland at the Château de Lançy near Geneva. After that the two boys lived in Paris for six months with Mrs. Williams and William was enrolled at the Lycée Condorcet. Later, after Williams had secured his medical degree at the University of Pennsylvania in 1906, he was again able to have a year of study abroad, this time one of postgraduate medical work at the University of Leipzig. Whether an inner sense of rootlessness possessed Williams because of a background which must have seemed exotic to Rutherford is worth considering. It is true his parents had been among the founders of the first Unitarian Church in the town, that they were respected and even outstanding members of the community. Still, the young man with a foreign middle name, of "the dark Spanish beauty" described in his University yearbook, a mother who sometimes spoke Spanish and sometimes an imperfect English, must have faced at some stage in his development the interesting question of just what he was in fact to *be,* if he *were,* in the first place, an American.

But as artist these insecurities were translated to another impulse, perhaps equally connected with "belonging," but freed of the programmatic impurities which, Brooks, for example, was bringing to bear on his researches. Williams wished to get at the inner meaning of America through possessing her present. It was the present, the thick, living flux of the present he wished to fix and "raise to the imagination." On the political level, this need was being expressed by critics such as Randolph Bourne and others of the Seven Arts group of which Bourne was the most brilliant theoretician. But the practicing aesthetic of this search for a significant America had, for the most part, been left to the regional folk-poets like Lindsay and Sandburg, and the neo-Freudian impressionism of Sherwood Anderson. Lindsay and Sandburg drew heavily on folk materials; Anderson got perverse sustenance from the varied stigmata of small-town life in America, those stigmata of personality composed into his moving Gothic "Grotesques."

There is no doubt that Williams profited from these investigations but he was not the man to take a position on authority. The quality of his own investigation of the American "now" was not anything the regionalists would have endorsed. They would have been unsympathetic to Williams' preoccupation with technique as at once a means and an end for a specifically American poetry. Sandburg's loose, slow-moving, Whitmanian free-verse cadences, arranged like prose paragraphs, and cemented together by refrains, reveal little awareness of technical responsibility.

The regionalists, both in prose and poetry, were basically concerned with content. For Williams there was no dichotomy whatever. For him, as earlier with Poe, the formal problem *was* the American problem. To create a new poetry in the American language, a new modus of representation was needed as well. Thinking back to his writings in 1912, one remembers his original preoccupation with form. The early historical plays, as we shall see, absorbed a concurrent interest in the character of the American past. Still, the times as well as his reliance on himself as the arbiter of the *how to do* was forcing upon him more and more the question of what to do it to. In short, his aesthetic increasingly demanded the closest organic relation between form and content.

The opening poem of *Al Que Quiere!*, the much anthologized "Sub Terra," dramatizes the prevailing mood of the collection:

> Where shall I find you,
> you my grotesque fellows
> that I seek everywhere
> to make up my band?
> None, not one
> with the earthy tastes I require;
> the burrowing pride that rises
> subtly as on a bush in May.
>
> . . .
>
> You to come with me
> poking into negro houses
> with their gloom and smell!
> In among children

leaping around a dead dog!
Mimicking
onto the lawns of the rich!
You!
to go with me a-tip-toe,
head down under heaven,
nostrils lipping the wind!

The "grotesque fellows . . . with the earthy tastes" are found, found in the poet's imagination as he frolics into the living world (a world which includes dead things, like the dog) under his heels, and which he transfigures by his clarity and well-being.

The best poems in *Al Que Quiere!* follow the lead of "Sub Terra." They are united by a common appeal—the appeal to open the eyes wide on what is before us, to accept, and to find joy in the acceptance. The improvisations played on this theme are various: "Pastoral" is a rejection of the common standards of "success" like the "Episcopal minister approaching the pulpit of a Sunday," in favor of the ". . . old man who goes about gathering dog-lime" and whose ". . . tread is more majestic . . ." The contrast between the obscure and the prominent, the powerful and the powerless is more overt than in later work, inclining tenderly toward the powerless long before the "proletarians" were to claim Williams. "Apology" continues the comparison and praises "The beauty of the terrible faces of our nonentities." "Gulls," by means of a parable of three gulls whom a circling eagle does not attack, breathes a humble but passionate plea for mutual tolerance between the "singer" and his "townspeople."

THE POEMS

There is a rich extension of the relationship between the
gulls and the eagle to the people in the great world who
"whirr" about the poet "calling, calling!"

In "Tract," perhaps the most memorable poem of this
volume, the poet again seeks to act as mediator between
custom and spirit:

> I will teach you my townspeople
> how to perform a funeral

The movement of this poem in its plain, walking tread,
free of metaphor, simple and unembellished, reflects a
dignified grief fitting to death, a grief commensurate ". . .
with some show/of inconvenience; sit openly—/to the
weather as to grief./Or do you think you can shut grief
in?" The gravity of the injunction weights the measure;
let death be its own comment:

> A rough plain hearse then
> with gilt wheels and no top at all,
> On this the coffin lies
> by its own weight.

In "Foreign" and "History," neither of which Williams
has seen fit to include in his *Complete Collected Poems*,
he continues his address to his townspeople. "Foreign,"
written in that charming vein of domestic spoofing at
which Williams excels, is more successful than "History"
which tries for a too-obvious irony to be wrung from the
juxtaposition of a decayed Christianity and a vital pagan
culture.

Flowing from these considerations of the poet's own
function and *place* in relation to the locality in which he

must move and live, are a group of poems somewhat more
objective in tone, in which people in the poet's community
are allowed to speak for themselves. The formal means in
this group is first person monologue as opposed to the
hortatory cast of the first group where second person
singular address makes for a directness, immediacy and
urgency appropriate to the pleas, tracts, and apologies of
which it is composed. When that address is extended to
animals and even inanimate objects the effect is one of
an affectionate whimsicality.

Williams often uses a more objective monologue form
to accommodate the colorful material got in his daily work
as a doctor. "A Portrait of a Woman in Bed" is a succinct
study of hostility and despair. The brusque speech of the
down-at-heels, bitter slut whom the doctor has come to
care for is remarkable for the way it mirrors her own
shortness toward life and society:

> I won't work
> and I've got no cash.
> What are you going to do
> about it?
> —and no jewelry
> (the crazy fools)
>
> But I've two eyes
> and a smooth face
> and here's this! look!
> it's high!
> . . .
>
> Try to help me
> if you want trouble
> or leave me alone
> that ends trouble.
> . . .

THE POEMS

While the poem might be termed a character study, it also functions as narrative and drama. We learn about the woman's children, her encounter with the county physician who last came, and sense the dramatic interaction of her criticism of the visiting doctor. The joylessness of her social defiance is communicated without a single interpretive comment in the crude flatness of the closing stanza:

> You could have closed the door
> when you came in;
> do it when you go out.
> I'm tired.

Drawing on this same area of experience, "Sympathetic Portrait of a Child," about "The murderer's little daughter," is moving both as an individual psychological study and as a social indictment which in the last stanza swiftly involves us all in a collective guilt for her plight. This is effected by the sudden introduction of the poet himself into the poem:

> Why has she chosen me
> for the knife
> that darts along her smile?

The suggestiveness of "darts," its aptness in summarizing the furtive quality of a felt but not understood guilt in the frightened little creature, sets up just the right tension between pathos and a potential hostility in its object. It leaves the matter delicately suspended between a right and wrong which is socially imposed, but nevertheless felt by the technically innocent child. The exterior frame of realistic "portrait" and the use of the present tense contribute to a direct vision of the child.

It is useful to notice how often in this collection, Williams relies on the method of portraiture. "Canthara," "M. B.," "Danse Russe," and "The Ogre," among others, are portraits and sometimes, as in the last two, self-portraiture. Since Williams at this time and, indeed, all through his life was keenly alive to contemporary art (he was the close friend of leading American painters like Stuart Davis, Marsden Hartley, Charles Demuth, Hilaire Hiler, Charles Sheeler, and others), whose interests, for the most part, exclude portraiture, we must infer that his use of the portrait is not an academic one. Still, Williams may have implied a bold literality in his usage, one defined by the angular, many-faceted and multi-surfaced areas of interest and textural relationship by which a modern painter's approach to "portraiture" is described. Applying this concept to "The Ogre" we see that the portrait is composed of the various levels of consciousness which are accessible to an adult man and a little girl. The sexual prescience of the child is used by the "ogre" as a rationale of the thoughts he would "put over and under and around" her.

Somewhat the same double function of the poet as at once the detached spectator and the guilty conscience of society is achieved in the tender "The Old Men," another portrait, this time of those "cut from touch":

> I bow my head in shame
> for those who malign you.
> Old men
> The peaceful beer of impotence
> be yours.

THE POEMS

In "Canthara," a portrait of an "old black-man," Williams again demonstrates his insight into age, especially into the problem of sensuality in old age which only Yeats in our time has stated more profoundly.

"A Portrait in Greys" is portraiture more at the metaphysical level, or, rather, at the level of epistemology. It represents the ambivalence between polar states of the self and the anti-self. There is a certain obscurity to the referents which leaves the poem without much semantic anchorage. There is the person in grey and the one "moving counter to you." In spite of the reader's uncertainty as to who "the one" really is, the narrator yet sees himself as somehow succored and borne up by this dim figure.

> I
> standing upon your shoulders touching
> a grey, broken sky—
> but you, weighted down with me,
> yet gripping my ankles,—move
> laboriously on.

The artist in this poem is viewed as a grotesque, a Siamese twin of venality and aspiration.

But more often at this time Williams celebrated the joyous, liberating function of the creative act. "January Morning," a long poem, which Williams subtitled a "Suite" (although it is rather a suite of tableaux than of musical compositions), is a clearly autobiographical account of the habits of a young doctor-artist whose work calls him to be about at "the strange hours" which yield beauty, just as "the beauties of travel are due to the strange hours we keep to see them." The spectacle of a man enjoying what he does in the way of work is one of the easist ways

23

to effect pleasure in the onlooker. Williams' *joie de vivre*
is infectious:

> the young girls run giggling
> on Park Avenue after dark
> when they ought to be home in bed
> Well,
> That's the way it is with me, somehow.

In the bold "Danse Russe" this *joie de vivre* is intensi-
fied until it arrives at a representation of the narcissistic
element in all creation. The poem is arresting for the
manner in which it fuses Williams' domestic vein (just
getting into its stride in *Al Que Quiere!*) with the portrait-
of-the-artist motif. The swift, weaving, repetitive measures
as they build up a mood of nocturnal frisking enhance
the tone of speculative intimacy:

> If I when my wife is sleeping
> and the baby and Kathleen
> are sleeping
> and the sun is a flame-white disc
> in silken mists
> above shining trees,—
> if I in my north room
> dance naked, grotesquely
> before my mirror
> waving my shirt round my head
> and singing softly to myself:
> "I am lonely, lonely.
> I was born to be lonely,
> I am best so!"
> If I admire my arms, my face
> my shoulders, flanks, buttocks
> against the yellow drawn shades,—
>
> Who shall say I am not
> the happy genius of my household?

THE POEMS

No other poet of our time has made domesticity, the arts of the home, more aesthetically meaningful than Williams. The domestic strain of "Good-Night" anticipates Williams' masterpiece in this domain, "This Is Just to Say." The conflict in "Good-Night" is a simply stated one: the present reality (parsley in the kitchen) versus the reality of memory, "memory playing the clown" (the ballet slippers of the girls in crimson satin). Parsley wins but it wins, let us note, *aesthetically:* "Parsley in a glass, still and shining, brings me back . . ." This is an important victory. But like all conquest it is temporary. It will be interesting to observe on what terms the conflict is concluded in Williams' work two decades later. *A Dream of Love,* we shall find, is the fullest exploration of the paradox of the artist as a domestic man.

Finally, in a poem modestly entitled "To a Solitary Disciple," a poem which could even now serve as epigraph to handbooks for poets, Williams, summing up the gains in craft "*Al Que Quiere!*" itself documents, instructs the would-be poet to observe his materials in terms of design, weight, texture and formal dynamics rather than in conventional color relationships and exotic metaphors. The poem is a humorous lesson in aesthetics, although one with a less social cast than Pound's delightful "A Lesson in Aesthetics." It is likely that Williams here was not merely instructing a novice, but taking formal leave of the Imagists as well:

> Rather notice, mon cher,
> that the moon is
> tilted above
> the point of the steeple

than that its color
is shell-pink.

Rather observe
that it is early morning
than that the sky
is smooth
as a turquoise.

Rather grasp
how the dark
converging lines
of the steeple
meet at the pinnacle—
perceive how
its little ornament
tries to stop them—

See how it fails!
See how the converging lines
of the hexagonal spire
escape upward—
receding, dividing!
—sepals
that guard and contain
the flower!

Observe
how motionless
the eaten moon
lies in the protecting lines.

It is true:
in the light colors
of morning
brown-stone and slate
shine orange and dark blue.

THE POEMS

> But observe
> the oppressive weight
> of the squat edifice!
> Observe
> the jasmine lightness
> of the moon.

Looking back, *Al Que Quiere!* seems a landmark in Williams' development. It announces in no uncertain terms the themes which would henceforth occupy him and suggests the special tone he was to take toward them. For Williams early practiced what Hawthorne had meant when he wrote ". . . thoughts are frozen and utterance benumbed unless the speaker stand in some true relationship with his audience . . ." The poet's widening interest in his immediate locality makes possible an extension of the social types in his portrait gallery. Yet there is no loss of intensity in the depiction. Williams' attitude toward society exhibits a Stendhalian objectivity of interest which has no connection with a vulgar naturalism. As it was Stendhal's sense of wonder which kept his minute reports from vulgarity, so it is the freshness of vision with which Williams attends his suburban dramatis personae that distinguishes these small but authentic witnesses from the crassness of their environment. While the titles are of a traditional kind (there are four Portraits, three Pastorals, three Love Songs) the cast of the poems themselves is not. A growing awareness of social hypocrisy and class tensions is the only sign *Al Que Quiere!* gives of having been written in the climate of the first World War.

· · · ·

When in 1920 the Four Seas Company published Williams' *Kora in Hell: Improvisations,* it begged the question of just what the book was by referring to it as "rhythmic prose." Actually, the poet had made clear in perhaps the longest prologue on literary record what he considered these compositions:

The true value [in art] is that peculiarity which gives an object a character by itself . . .

The imagination goes from one thing to another . . . But the thing that stands eternally in the way of really good writing is always one: the virtual impossibility of lifting to the imagination those things which lie under the direct scrutiny of the senses, close to the nose. It is this difficulty that sets a value upon all works of art and makes them a necessity. The senses witnessing what is immediately before them in detail see a finality which they cling to in despair, not knowing which way to turn . . .

I thought at first to adjoin to each improvisation a more or less opaque commentary. But the mechanical interference that would result makes this inadvisable. Instead I have placed some of them in the preface where without losing their original intention . . . they relieve the later text and also add their weight to my present fragmentary argument . . .

I have placed the following Improvisations in groups somewhat after the ABA formula, that one may support the other, clarifying or enforcing perhaps the other's attention.

This was the "notes" era in poetry: Marianne Moore was using them; Eliot had yet to do his bibliographical exegesis of *The Waste Land.* Williams has notes separated from the text of each poem by a small ruled line after Metastasio's habit in his *Varie Poesie* (1795). The Prologue, it should be noted, is dated 1918, Williams' thirty-fifth year. The book itself was not published until two years later. Williams apparently wished it had not been published at all, for he did not include a single one of the Improvisations in either the *Collected Poems* or the *Complete Collected Poems*. As early as 1921, *Improvisations* had been written down as a failure even by Williams' admirers. Kenneth Burke, for example, in reviewing *Sour Grapes*, says of the *Improvisations* that they "were not finally satisfactory. Clear notes were there in abundance, but they were usually preceded and followed by the usual modern data for mental tests." The most penetrating and enthusiastic reception of *Kora in Hell* was to come from a French source—almost a decade later in René Taupin's *L'Influence du Symbolisme Français sur la Poésie Américaine*.

Twenty-five years later it is possible to agree with Burke's evaluation of the *Improvisations* but it is impossible to dismiss them as merely a temporary aberration of the poet, who, after that, has a remission and returns to sanity in his next book. For, in spite of the extreme position Williams takes in this curious book, it provides valuable cues and sources for his later direction. And, quite on its own terms, it provides some incidental beauties. It is now unimportant to ask whether these short stanza-paragraphs are "rhythmic prose" (publisher's version), "poems" (poet's version), or just plain "prose" (the critics' version). They are not "poems" in the sense of the poet's own earlier and later work. They may be "prose with a heightened consciousness"—to borrow Marianne Moore's definition of Hebrew poetry. However we choose to classify them, today their interest is primarily illustrative and historical. The fact that Williams wrote prose commentaries for them, as a means of reinforcing the "fragmentary" argument, indicates that he must have been suspicious of their status and communicability as poetry.

The Prologue is the most instructive part of *Improvisations*. It is so much a document of its time for the way in which it reflects what were then the "live options" in writing that it is worth examining with some care. It includes, as well, some interesting communications from H.D., Ezra Pound and Wallace Stevens. Williams' reiteration that "Nothing is good save the new" leads him here to some extravagant conclusions: "If a thing have novelty it stands intrinsically beside every other work of artistic excellence." What Williams really meant by this dangerously inclusive judgment was better expressed in another passage: "It is in the continual and violent refreshing of the idea that love and good writing have their security." Unfortunately, however, Williams did not juxtapose the two propositions, and thus qualify them. Instead, he was led on to an irritable although telling attack on Eliot and the Prufrock typology. It is to this somewhat exacerbated critique that I should trace the dislike Williams engendered in Eliot, and in the latter's British and American disciples. Mr. Eliot's comment some years later to the effect that Williams was a poet of some local significance is still, I suspect, the received British view on Williams, although I am certain that were a new generation of poets to read him freshly they would find much to admire.

Williams, depending on the touchstone of the "new" finds even "Eliot's more exquisite work is rehash, repetition in another way of Verlaine, Baudelaire, Maeterlinck —conscious or unconscious—just as there were Pound's

early paraphrases from Yeats and his constant later crib-
bing from the Renaissance, Provence and the modern
French: men content with the connotations of their masters." Williams, annoyed because a British critic had
deemed Prufrock a "new world" type, contends that "Prufrock, the nibbler at sophistication, is endemic in every
capital . . ." He attacks the British critic for his endorse-
ment of Eliot's "La Figlia Que Piange" as "the very fine
flower of the finest spirit of the United States" (truly an
inept observation!), on the grounds that "the poem con-
forms . . . just the right amount of everything drained
through . . ." Similar criticisms have since been made of
this poem but no one was making them in 1918. Unfortunately, Williams had no instinct for the politic tone
and here, as elsewhere in his early critical prose, a too
personal invective embarrasses the sound judgment.

In reality, what Williams was opposed to in Eliot
and Pound was not so much the manner as the whole direction, trend, and philosophic import of their work. It
seems fairly clear from *Al Que Quiere!* that Williams
was already formulating a program for himself which
reaffirmed a romantic Emersonian ethic of self-reliance
translated to the aesthetic sphere.

But in spite of Williams' confidence in his aesthetic independence it was possible a decade later for a perceptive French critic, M. René Taupin, to see the *Improvisations* as the heir of Rimbaud's *Illuminations*. More
radically, M. Taupin argues, Williams from the early
days of his Imagism was responding to the French Sym-
bolist tradition in poetry and to contemporary French
painters like Duchamp, Gris and others whose work Wil-

liams was championing when their names were unknown in America. Williams was partially indebted to these sources for his great precision of observation as well as his liberation of emotion through the joyous translation of the real world into the world of the spirit. Ranking Williams as one of the three greatest American poets, M. Taupin raises the question, "Perhaps Williams has composed the formula for American art?"

In the *Improvisations* Taupin sees Williams abandoning the prosodic limitations of the Imagists and pushing his explorations further in the direction of the "organized" dream material of Rimbaud and his Surrealist descendents. Williams "has completed the work of Pound and Eliot in an entirely personal fashion. He has not discovered a new force in literature, that which Pound and Eliot had done so admirably. But he has vitalized the emotions to a point which no one had reached in American literature . . . Williams knows more about the poetic imagination than any American poet today." And while his art does not suffer from being compared to the Symbolists, and especially that of Rimbaud (M. Taupin persuasively documents the latter connection with parallel quotations from *Illuminations* and *Improvisations*) yet his sensibility is peculiarly American and may be compared to that of Marianne Moore and perhaps that of Henry James. "Ils ont tous cette vie des sens qui s'exasperent sur le contact de choses, qui les saisissent comme un courant électrique. Chacque rapture est une douleur aussi bien que l'obsession que devient ce contact: entre les deux extrêmes, il y a la joie, et le plaisir de vivre . . ."

Philosophically, it is Rimbaud whom Williams is echoing. " 'Il faut se faire voyant,' disait Rimbaud. 'Il faut prendre contact,' dit Williams." Williams' central image of the "Dance" in the *Improvisations* was an image dear to Rimbaud, as well, and stood for the free and joyous movement of the intellect.[1]

While M. Taupin's thesis may seem to us now as unduly conditioned by his closeness in time to the technical revolutions he was describing, as well as by the wish to claim the poets he admired for France, it is nevertheless valuable to have a serious critic quite *outside* the nationalities, parties, movements and commitments of the poetry of 1910–1920 judging the so different work of Eliot, Pound and Williams as yet part of a larger tendency to reject the reigning English tradition through a common dislocation of language. In the same way, Baudelaire, Rimbaud, Mallarmé and Cocteau had forced a dislocation which made the vocabulary of French poetry appropriate to the expression of new things. If we find this conclusion too sweeping, we must remind ourselves that the first decade of the renascence in poetry was more responsive to hints from abroad than was the next one. In Williams' case, as in the others, the obligations after the early twenties were to be different. Indeed, we can now see *Improvisations* as the preparation for a new poetic modus in his work.

Perhaps Ezra Pound was the first to recognize, in his patronizing way, where Williams was heading. He saw that Williams was not travelling the cosmic Whitmanian

---

[1] This discussion is based especially on pp. 278–290 of *L'Influence du Symbolisme Français sur La Poésie Américaine.*

route which the mid-western mystics of regionalism, Lindsay, Masters and Sandburg were selling at popular prices:

> . . . Would H., with the swirl of the prairie wind in her underwear, or the virile Sandburg recognize you, an effete easterner as a REAL American? INCONCEIVABLE!!!!! . . .
> You have the native credulity of a County Clare emigrant. . . .
> Of course, Sandburg will tell you that you miss the "big drifts" and Bodenheim will object to your not being sufficiently decadent. . . .
> The thing that saves your work is opacity, and don't forget it. Opacity is NOT an American quality.

Pound was right about Williams' opacity as it applied to his "American" quality. When the twenty-seven *Improvisations* have been read one looks back vainly for an "American" motif. But America nevertheless gets in "opaquely" by using precisely what is at hand for poetic investigation. And what is at hand is just as often pennyroyal, mushrooms, clouds or mallows as it is a fragmentary landscape of motor cars catching fleeting vistas of a broken beauty and breeze-echoed fragments of speech. There are the quick tableaux of "the little Polish Father of Kingsland," of "Hercules in Hacketstown doing farm labor," of the married suburbanites each secretly yearning for a magic release from one another yet none capable of a gesture toward fulfillment, of the Sunday church bells, of the Doctor who sees disease and corruption in the blood and yet sings of a joyous deliverance, of the burlesque show girls, of a nocturnal childbirth. What interests Williams in these variegated fragments of a common society is suggested by the prose commentary of *Improvisation X:* "You would learn—if you knew even one city—where people are a little gathered together and

34

where one sees—it's our frontier you know—the common changes of the human spirit."

But antecedent to these studies are the interesting speculations on the nature of art and the artist which is developed from various points of view all through the *Improvisations*. It is this superb exploration—not resolution —of the problems of creation which is the real achievement of the book, rather than the too-splintered studies of Americana. Williams should have known that a poem is not "composed" by the mere contiguity of details. When Williams considers old and new ways (poetically speaking) of getting at "reality" he is more successful. The interplay between the "imaginative qualities of actual things" and the perceiving imagination is thought of as a kind of slow dance, interpreting as it moves. The notion of the universal mythic qualities of actual concrete things is applied in the instance of modern deities we do not recognize:

Zeus is a country doctor without a taste for coin jingling . . . that girl, you know, the one that should have been Venus by the lust that's in her. They've got her down there among the railroad men. A crusade couldn't rescue her. Up to jail—or call it down to Limbo —the Chief of Police our Pluto. It's all of the gods, there's nothing else worth writing of . . . They are the same men as they always were—but fallen. Do they dance now, they that danced beside Helicon. They dance much as they did then, only, few have an eye for it, through the dirt and fumes.

This "fallen" Olympiad is the nucleus out of which Williams was years later to compose the triumphantly indigenous myth of *Paterson*.

In the end, then, a "poem can be made of anything; the

act is disclosed by the imagination of it . . . the imagination leads and the deed comes behind." But the poet even if he is not a country doctor, officiating at a nocturnal childbirth, sees the act and the "imagination" of it from whatever *situ* in society he happens to occupy. Thus Williams' ambivalence in valuation establishes in effect a counterpoint between the ideal and the real (the poetic and the anti-poetic, if you will) in experience. Williams' daily work as a physician provides an opportunity for this kind of scrutiny in the most dramatic terms. The violent antitheses of death and decay, over against reproduction and renewal, play an antiphonal chant for recognition in his consciousness. In terms of art that is what Williams means when he writes, cryptically, "After thirty years of staring at one true phrase he discovered that its opposite was true also." To such a sensibility "one is a ridiculous savior of the poor with fatigue always at his elbow . . ." But no matter how treacherous, a man must place his center of value in art for "After some years of varied experience with the bodies of the rich and the poor a man finds little to distinguish between them, bulks them as one and bases his working judgments on other matters."

In spite of the quiet power of these meditations there is at times a certain defiant and self-conscious posing. We see Williams in a conventional "poetic" domino, a sprite, a pixie, a brave nose-thumbing fellow, an alchemist or wizard of logic; in short, as artistically a little more and humanly a little less than the poet need claim for himself.

Improvisations for all its memorable pictures, its incisive exploration of the artist's job of work is, in total effect, a diary of interior conflict. It is illuminating to know that Williams wrote one Improvisation each night for a whole year, no matter how fatigued from his medical practice "anything that came, not into my head, but from my writing hand." Perhaps this explains why as a source book for Williams' attitudes during this period it is valuable, while as a sustained work of art it seems to us now, as it eventually did to Williams, inadequate and callow in its stylized violence. Still, as a therapy for externalizing some of the conflicts that then disturbed him, this violence had its salutary effects. Williams' next poems show a new composure and balance.

. . . .

When *Sour Grapes* appeared in 1921 Williams already had a devoted if small following among the most brilliant young literary men in the country. One of them, Kenneth Burke, writing in *The Dial* paid Williams the dangerous compliment of endorsing certain qualities of his work as if they represented its entirety:

. . . What Williams sees he sees in a flash . . . No, Williams is the master of the glimpse. A line of his . . . will throw the reader into unexpected intimacy with his subject, like pushing open a door into some foreign face . . . It would be mere idleness to give his *ars poetica* in more presumptuous terms. The process is simply this: There is the eye, and there is the thing upon which the eye alights; while the relationship existing between the two is a poem.

Karl Shapiro's uncritical use of this idea some twenty-five years later can be found in his shallow study of modern poetics, *Essay in Rime*.

But it was by the "philosophical" reduction of Williams' position as stated in the Manifesto to *Contact*, a magazine which Williams was then editing with Robert McAlmon, that Burke "placed" Williams in a way which continues to define him for the intellectually dependent. Burke declared:

I take contact to mean: man without the syllogism, without the parody, without Spinoza's ethics, man with nothing but the thing and the feeling of that thing . . . Seen from this angle, Contact might be said to resolve into the counterpart of Culture, and Williams becomes thereby one of our most distinguished Neanderthal men . . . His hatred of the idea in art is consequently pronounced, and very rightly brings in its train a complete disinterest in form . . . Williams, however, must go back to the source. And the process undeniably has its beauties.

While Burke's perception of some qualities in Williams is admirable, he shows here the same brilliant irresponsibility which has made his more ambitious critical studies at once suggestive and suspect. Burke, "the man of ideas" in literature, is always impelled to abstract his *ad hoc* observations into universals, into epigrammatic charts which falsify rather than illuminate his particular insights. In regard to Williams, Burke has foundered on a spurious identification of form and idea. To reject "ideas," if this is Williams' heresy, is not to reject form, order, in the creative act. In reality, it is merely the *sanction* of systems which Williams rejects in favor of a perhaps naïve hope that without them the artist may see things anew and order them freshly. *Contact* urged the criticism of ideas by re-directing them to the things they were said to express but often obscured. This point of view is comparable to the position taken by Herbert Read in *To Hell With Culture* and in *Poetry and Anarchism* which I shall discuss in connection with Williams' fiction.

When one looks at *Sour Grapes,* unencumbered by touchstones, it becomes clear that it is more intimately connected with *Al Que Quiere!* (1917) than with *Improvisations* (1920). In *Sour Grapes* there is a greater economy of line and a closer restriction to the description of the concrete fact in its own terms. Still, there seeps through a certain self-absorption which subtly invades the integrity of the effect. Themes carried over from *Al Que Quiere!* thus acquire new overtones. The tender compassion for the aged communicated so persuasively in "Canthara" now becomes an almost compulsive lament, with minute spillings of nuance in the direction of the poet himself.

In "Time the Hangman" a recognition of the meaning of old age is reached by the method of contrast. Similarly, in the passionate "Lament of the Widow in Springtime," a poem written about Williams' mother and one which has received high praise from critics, again develops a poignant antithesis in the barrenness of the widow and the fruition of the natural world about her. In "To Waken an Old Lady" the sensual frugality of old age "is a flight of small cheeping birds skimming bare trees, above a snow glaze." The restless atmosphere of this collection, underground, but exhaled as a scent about the words, seems to stem from a growing sense of the monotony of routinized work and domesticity. This is felt in "Good-Night," in "Complaint," a compressed narrative of the country doctor's mercy work of the night, and in "To A

Friend," a poem about a poet who is torn by his desire for women in the belief that

> . . . There is
> no good in the world except out of
> a woman and certain women alone
> for certain things.

The age-weighted "Waiting" concerns the guilt of one who has ceased to love his wife:

> Let us see, let us see!
> What did I plan to say to her
> When it should happen to me
> as it has happened now.

Sometimes this pervasive sense of age, death, decay is objectified more strictly, as in "Approach of Winter," where the fact of sterility is bitterly anchored in the natural world with a dry precision of detail. This poem should be read next to "The Desolate Field" or "January" in which the natural world is seen not as facsimile of man's inner progress toward death, but as an antagonist against whose invasions man pits his desire and will to believe in the future. The bare, dehumanized description of "Approach of Winter" in its hardness, compactness, lack of metaphor, presages with admirable control what was later to be named by Williams and his friends the "Objectivist" method. There is only one subjective, evaluatory phrase in the whole poem: the salvias, "hard carmine" are said to be "like no leaf that ever was." Curiously, it is the weight of "like no leaf that ever was" which pulls together the powerfully literal terms of the poem to make it *more* than a picture of winter (age).

THE POEMS

Just so in "The Red Wheelbarrow," it is the line "so much depends" which creates the "tone" of that much anthologized gem, and raises it from a merely brilliant *hokku*-type tableau to the backyard paradise of a new aesthetic. But it is the now well-known "Complete Destruction" which states most uncompromisingly in its monosyllabic brutality the thing which Williams was to say again and again but with increasing power and richness, about death-in-life and life-in-death:

> It was an icy day.
> We buried the cat,
> then took her box
> and set match to it
>
> in the back yard.
> Those fleas that escaped
> earth and fire
> died by the cold.

A cluster of poems in this collection continues Williams' delicate evocation of beauty in the natural world. Pieces like "The Tulip Bed" and "Blue Flags," in their dynamic factuality of flowers lead one to agree with Wallace Stevens' dictum that there is no one who writes more exquisitely of flowers. In "A Celebration" ("This day has blossomed long enough") and in "April" ("I had no rest against that springtime!") the beauty of the natural world, again seen in terms of flowers, is so intense the poet is fatigued by the demands they make upon his sensibility: "Flowers are a tiresome pastime."

In "Willow Poem," "The Late Singer," "Blizzard," "Spring Storm," "Daisy," "Primrose" and "Queen Ann's

Lace" the interaction of nature with human event is implicit. It is in the joyously direct indirection of "Primrose" which begins:

> Yellow, yellow, yellow!
> It is not a color.
> It is summer!

It is in the hint of liberation, of the releasing of winter's hard fastnesses in "Spring Storm":

> The sky has given over
> its bitterness
> . . . .
>
> Still the snow keeps
> its hold on the ground
> But water, water
> from a thousand runnels!
> It collects swiftly,
> dappled with black
> cuts a way for itself
> through green ice in the gutters.

Sour Grapes invades the imagination with a lusty natural sweetness not at all suggested by its ironic title. The poet's attention is chiefly turned toward natural events at various levels of signification.

But a collection would not have been Williams' had it not flown from classification by a mischievous ambivalence of mood. Here, for example, the lie is given to our earlier suspicion of a wearying of domesticity by the arch words of "The Thinker" who talks to his wife's new pink slippers with their "gay pom-poms" in his "Secret mind out of pure happiness." Similarly, a balance for the preoccupation with old age is achieved by the insouciant "Light-

Hearted William," its sheer good health defining one of Williams' most likeable qualities:

> Light hearted William twirled
> his November mustaches
> and, half-dressed, looked
> from the bedroom window
> upon the spring weather
> . . .
>
> Into the room he drew
> his head again and laughed
> to be himself quietly
> twirling his green mustaches.

Yet in the intense "Portrait of the Author," a poem rescued from the wastebasket by the poet's friend, Robert Mc-Almon, he reverts to the introspective mood of *Improvisations* in an attempt to assimilate the terror of beauty when "Black is split at once into flowers."

. . . . .

By 1925 when *Spring and All* appeared, dedicated to Charles Demuth, the painter, Williams was affirming Spring instead of being terrorized by it. The acceptance of Spring, as the title suggests, includes an acceptance of "all" as well. The collection is a slender one with a running prose commentary of aesthetic in the manner of *Improvisations* but more pared-down and literal. In the *CCP* the titles used in *Spring and All* are omitted, the intention apparently being to stress relatedness by connecting the poems with numerals. The omission of the titles seems ill advised. As a whole, the volume shows a greater sensitivity to the modern world in terms of its surface composition: nitrogen, motor cars, garbage heaps, movie palaces, jazz and gin. Williams experiments with a kind of collage technique by which slogans, signs, advertisements, popular songs, menus, are cleverly juxtaposed to expose the banalities and shoddiness of the times. Hart Crane in *The Bridge* later borrowed some of these devices in the sections "Cutty Sark," "The River," and "The Tunnel."

In *Spring and All* one feels Williams is trying to clarify his own defenses, seeking to consolidate a position which will be as impregnable to his own quixotic ambivalence as to his enemies' assaults. Five years before, in *Kora in Hell*, Kora (Persephone), the muse, was in her winter captivity in Hades. Now, as Spring, her durance is over and she is above ground, free of confinement. What is sought, states the prose commentary, is to remove the

"constant barrier between the reader and his consciousness of immediate contact with the world . . .

. . . nearly all writing, up to the present, if not all art, has been especially designed to keep up the barrier between sense and the vaporous fringe which distracts the attention from its agonized approaches to the moment. It has always been a search for the beautiful illusion. . . . ᴛo whom then am I addressed? To the imagination." [2]

Williams wishfully envisions a holocaust (in "Chapters," some only three or four lines long) by which all forms and modes of life are destroyed and suddenly "It is spring; life again begins to assume its normal appearance as of today . . . THE WORLD IS NEW."

In this new world "The imagination, freed from the

[2] For purposes of clarity I have transposed the order of the quotation.

handcuffs of art takes the lead! Her feet are bare and not too delicate." But Williams is aware of the criticism the "traditionalists" would point at him for his "antipoetry," his "primitivism." He is aware that the jump from the stale "to Cezanne or back to certain of the primitives is the impossible." He defines his use of the term: "The primitives are not BEHIND experience. Work which bridges the gap between the rigidities of vulgar experience and the imagination is rare. It is new, immediate— It is so because it is actual, always real. It is experience dynamized into reality." And to secure this "pageless actual" in art, to compose it, crystallize it into "value," that is to say, a "separate existence," it is necessary in poetry to annihilate the "like," the metaphorical:

> Crude symbolism is to associate emotions with natural phenomena such as anger with lightning, flowers with love . . . Such work is empty . . . Everything that I have done in the past—except those parts which may be called excellent—by chance, have that quality about them.
>
> It is typified by use of the word "like" or that "evocation" of the "image" which served us for a time. Its abuse is apparent. The insignificant "image" may be "evoked" never so ably and still mean nothing . . .
>
> What I put down of value will have this value: an escape from crude symbolism, the annihilation of strained associations, complicated ritualistic forms designed to separate the work from "reality" —such as rhyme, meter as meter and not as the essential of the work, one of its words.

Spring and All keeps faith with Williams' announced aim. This does not mean that he is able to toss out, in a single sweep, all the learned habits of his earlier writing even were it desirable to do so. Poem XXVII (in *CCP,*

45

XXVIII) beginning "Black eyed Susan" in its simple, enumerative *contrast* with "white daisy" and crowds which "are white as farmers who live poorly" and in its simple, enumerative *likeness* to one "rich in savagery —Arab, Indian, dark woman" is, in spite of the resolution to abandon "likes," a "like" poem. This does not detract from its merits, which are, I think, typical of the best of Williams' by then discarded Imagism. The poem is superior to some "like" poems in that it is not so much a comparative statement of the qualities of savagery in the black-eyed Susan *as compared* to those in Arab, Indian or dark women, but rather a full identification (a more absolute method of image-making) of the flower with that kind of woman. This nominative coupling may be termed personification, but it is accomplished without the usual preliminary fuss. "Composition," a weak poem, also suggests a pictorial "Imagist" orientation.

The other poems, however, belong almost completely to Williams' "new world." The highly praised I, "By the road to the contagious hospital," a poem which Williams considers one of his best, and which Yvor Winters in *Primitivism and Decadence* terms "directed meditation," sets the tone for the majority of the poems. It is an invocation to that "new world" which *Spring and All* announced in the prose. The "new world" appears with a stripped and detached austerity in its own terms, here, those of landscape. I am not sure that I do not do the poem an injustice to allegorize it in the light of the prose commentary. The theme is clearly "the stark dignity of entrance." The "twiggy stuff of bushes and small trees" which

> . . . enter the new world naked,
> cold uncertain of all
> save that they enter.

I should not agree with Mr. Winters who makes a close but confused study of this poem in judging the feeling of the last two lines (of the eight which he thinks "central" to the poem) to be one of "pathos, aroused by the small and familiar in austere and unfriendly surroundings." The central and concluding lines are:

> Now the grass, tomorrow
> the stiff curl of wild carrot leaf

> One by one objects are defined—
> It quickens: clarity, outline of leaf

> But now the stark dignity of
> entrance—Still, the profound change
> has come upon them: rooted, they
> grip down and begin to awaken

It is not "pathos" which summarizes the tone of these lines but rather the sense of an heroic labor as necessary to even the smallest event of birth, or awakening. The "small and familiar" seen in terms of struggle and difficulty sets up not pathos but muted agony as the mood. Similarly, I should question Mr. Winters' brief reference to the metrical structure of this poem, although on different grounds. They rest in my inability to accept Mr. Winters' scheme of scansion as it is developed elsewhere in *Primitivism and Decadence*. And I am interested to find that Mr. R. P. Blackmur also cannot follow the discussion of Williams' free verse ". . . preferring to believe that Dr. Williams' astonishing success comes from the combination of a good ear for speech cadence and for the balance of meaning and sound, plus a faculty for the double effect of weight and speed." [3]

I am puzzled to unravel Mr. Winters' simultaneous descriptions of Williams as one of "the masters of free verse," "a primitive" (and thus a "Decadent") and though "an experimental poet by virtue of his meter, . . . in other qualities of his language one of the most richly traditional poets of the past hundred and fifty years; in fact, making allowance for his somewhat narrow scope one would be tempted to compare him, in this respect, to such poets as Hardy and Bridges." [4] I cannot feel that this series of contradictory labels has brought the reader nearer to an understanding of what actually goes on in Williams poetry.

Poem III continues the birth motif of "By the road to the contagious hospital" but here a Hardyesque figure is introduced:

> Down past the brushwood
> bristling by
> the rainsluiced wagonroad
> looms the artist figure of
> the farmer—composing
> —antagonist

The ironic ambiguity of the farmer's relation to nature, his need to make order, and his limitations in fighting disorder (the invasions of nature), it is this which raises the poem from a tableau to a rich moral perception of the meaning of making anything.

Several poems in *Spring and All,* and some of the very best, are records of the conflict in remaining faithful to

---

[3] *The Expense of Greatness,* p. 235.
[4] *Primitivism and Decadence,* especially pp. 67–71.

the intentions enunciated in the prose. Williams rejects the customary poetic roles assigned to night and day:

> . . . Nothing
> is gained by saying the night breeds
> murder—it is the classical mistake

It is because of the same process of false analogy that "boxing matches and/Chinese poems are the same." To this kind of forced metaphor, Williams opposes a simple affirmation of the brute data of experience: "There is nothing in the twist of the wind but dashes of cold rain." And in a mood of plaintive confessional, the poem concludes:

> How easy to slip
> into the old mode, how hard to
> cling firmly to the advance—

Williams continues in this vein with a blanket rejection of "everything I have done," and in VII, a beautiful lyric is made out of one specific rejection of "tradition," "The rose is obsolete." [5]

> The rose carried weight of love
> but love is at an end—of roses

---

[5] Unnumbered (apparently in error) in original edition. The prose background of this poem, stemming from a discussion of the painter, Juan Gris, whom Williams much admired but whose work, at the time, he had not yet seen in color, clarifies it: ". . . the attempt is being made to separate things of the imagination from life, and obviously, by using the forms common to experience so as not to frighten the onlooker away but to invite him." In the poem the obsolete rose invites the onlooker to a contemplation of its imaginative life at its petals' edge from which a line penetrates to the Milky Way.

And yet a new poem can be made about a rose, by spinning out its own fragile organic structure, rather than the weight of its historical associations.

In VIII (felicitously titled "At the Faucet of June" in the *CP*) the writing problem is considered from yet another angle: How to reconcile the poetic and the anti-poetic? How to reconcile the classical past (anemones in Persephone's cow-pasture) with "J.P.M. . . . whose cars are about the finest on the market today . . . ?" But when this conflict is resolved, as in X, "The universality of things" draws the poet equally to the melon flowers and to the refuse about whose edges they open.

And, finally, in XXI, "The Red Wheelbarrow," that brilliant apotheosis of the "new world," a fresh, rain-washed universe of anti-poetic detail is composed into a moving whole by the simple ardor of the introductory line:

> so much depends
> upon
>
> a red wheel
> barrow
>
> glazed with rain
> water
>
> beside the white
> chickens

Here we get the full and concentrated weight of Williams' practice distilled into a quaintly deceptive primitivism of style which critics like to refer to as "Imagism" but which has little to do with that mode except for the intensely realized visual detail. It is the word "glazed" (texture),

"So much depends" (judgment), plus the isolation of "wheel" from "barrow" which graph the vivid evocation. For this last detail, it is useful to know of Williams' belief that since a word in a poem has two qualities, its meaning and its sound, while the line is a *unit* of sound-meaning relations, the poet may split a word any way he pleases.

In *Spring and All* it is in what I shall call the American poems that Williams departs from his earlier subject-matter and style. These poems introduce a different kind of "new world," a world thoroughly familiar to the modern reader, perhaps too familiar, so that he is divorced from any meaningful relation to it, until it is restated and composed for him through that address to the imagination which the prose of *Spring and All* invokes. I shall start with a consideration of one of the most extreme of these poems for it is one that seems to have puzzled both British and American critics. It precedes some of e. e. cummings' later phonetic transcription or, rather, rescriptions of American speech, summing up somewhat pyrotechnically both Williams' newly tight linear patterns and his growing preoccupation with American speech mores and cadences. The poem is extreme in the fidelity and not in the violence with which it seeks to represent, not reproduce, these patterns. An English critic,[6] following the lead of Laura Riding and Robert Graves in their earlier attack on Williams in *A Survey of Modernist Poetry* (1927), wrote of XVII in 1939, when it was reprinted in the *CCP*, that it was "typical" of Williams, "simple and confused, pointless and pretentious":

[6] Julian Symons, in the *New English Weekly*.

WILLIAM CARLOS WILLIAMS

Our orchestra
is the cat's nuts—

Banjo jazz
with a nickel plated

amplifier to
soothe

the savage beast—
Get the rhythm

That sheet stuff
's a lot of cheese.

Man
gimme the key

and lemme loose
I make 'em crazy

with my harmonies
Shoot it Jimmy

Nobody
Nobody else

but me—
They can't copy it

The critic leaves the quotation with "cheese" and as comment offers ". . . there is a period (the only one in the poem) after cheese," thus, incidentally, heightening the impression in the reader's mind that this is the whole poem! What is "confused, pointless, and pretentious" to Mr. Symons' ears seems economical, apt and admirably modest to mine. Must one go further? This delightful swagger of a monologue achieves exactly what it sets out to do. It is, in its smartly syncopated beat and in its catchy American idiom the testimonial of the "improvisateur" of jazz or swing, fixed for us in a shining context of his own making. The poem also serves as a modest example of the logical working out of what the Browning monologue technique offered for unsentimental use to the twentieth-century poet. The thing that has taken place in Williams' work between 1915 and 1923 is a greater bareness of suggestion for the reader to work with. The result in the realm of emotional control is, curiously, a greater precision of implication despite the apparent under-statement.

As for punctuation, it is not for the hell of it, as Mr. Symons suggests, that Williams has put a period after "cheese." It is because the thought and feeling alters at that point and with the following line "Man" we get an intensification and personalization of the general theme suggested by the opening lines down to "cheese." It is a definite contribution of Williams that he has recognized so painstakingly the importance of punctuation and typography to poetry. What e.e. cummings and others have also attempted in a more literal and (often) eccentric fashion, Williams has stabilized into a reliable and integral element in his technique.

The importance of the visual structure of poetry is not a trivial notion. So conscientiously does Williams take the matter of punctuation that, comparing the 1934 Objectivist Press edition of the *Collected Poems* with earlier versions, one finds emendations in which commas,

53

periods, spacing, capitals, etc., have been patiently juggled with increasing sharpness of impact as end-product. Titles, too, play an important role in Williams' poetry, and frequently as integral part of the poem. Sometimes, they are bi-functional, serving as titular or thematic emphases, and as first line of the poem as well, a practice sometimes employed by Marianne Moore.

For the most part, Williams' more characteristic violence lies in the clinical ruthlessness with which data are selected, as in the poignant sketch of the jaundiced old woman in XVI "rolling her saffron eyeballs" and crying "I can't die." Only a few details are given for the reader to construct this terrifying, almost too faithful evocation of the inevitable degradation of the body: the tongue "licking the sore on her nether lip" juxtaposed with the set-off line "O toppled belly" suggests the rigidly deterministic frame of implication. In dealing with old age in "Can-thara," Williams had made an explicit judgment of its quality, but now it is we who must evaluate. The single word "toppled" evokes not merely the belly now but the belly *before;* for in order to topple, a thing must have had firmness, substance. The toppled belly is perhaps the most brutal "anti-poetic" detail Williams could have selected to point up the de-sexualization of old age in a woman. It is the kind of detail perhaps only a physician who sees illustrated in his daily work over and over the growing conformance of the sexes to one another in old age could use. It reveals old age robbed of creative validity but not of the wish for it. The brutality of the paradox outlined by the poem will turn away all but experienced readers of verse, that is to say, all those who will not see the tragic fall symbolized by the debased body. It is the presence of this inner contrast which saves the poem from too great demands upon the reader's ability to "face facts." It is only if we can make "the jump between fact and imaginative reality" that the poem will succeed for us. For we are disposed to allow total destruction to the cat, but not to ourselves.

In the "American" group, XVIII (called "To Elsie" in the *CCP*) is a powerful poem which reappears twenty years later in *Paterson, Book I* in an altered form. The milieu of the earlier piece becomes the protagonist of the long poem. XVIII is a character study drawn through narrative, and also an elegiac lyric which laments the decline of natural vigor in the gaudy times of Elsie with "no peasant traditions to give them character." Elsie is a kind of Yeatsian "Crazy Jane" presented without Yeats' idealization of the desecrated woman as the authentic guarantor of some superior wholeness, an authenticity with which Yeats also endowed his fools and lunatics. Nor does Williams isolate Elsie from her social context as does Yeats his Crazy Jane. Williams holds before his vision a double Elsie: he can see her with "broken brain" expressing the truth about us

> her great ungainly hips and flopping breasts
>
> addressed to cheap
> jewelry
> and rich young men with fine eyes

but he also recognizes her as one of

> The pure products of America
> go crazy—
> mountain folk from Kentucky

> or the ribbed north end of
> Jersey
> with its isolate lakes and
>
> valleys, its deaf-mutes, thieves
> old names
> and promiscuity between
>
> devil-may-care men who have taken
> to railroading
> out of sheer lust of adventure
>
> and young slatterns, bathed
> in filth
> from Monday to Saturday

Elsie belongs to one of the "old names" in the ribbed north end of Jersey which are in some communities populated by the notorious Jackson Whites, the inbred off-spring of generations of descent from Hessian deserters of the Revolutionary War, Indians and Negroes. Williams has developed this investigation of the "pure products" of America on another level in his essay, "The First Families of Virginia." The two views of Elsie enunciated in the poem are resolved into a delicately poised antithesis. For Elsie is like the rest of us in the modern world "degraded prisoners/ destined/ to hunger until we eat filth/ while the imagination strains/ after deer/"

> No one
> to witness
> and adjust, no one to drive the car

The utter hopelessness of Elsie, both victim and agent of her degraded circumstance, is connected with the more universal frustration of modern man, lacking the means of communication which alone reward the efforts of imagination, lacking the agency of control ("No one to drive the car") which validates these efforts. It is this theme of "no language" along with the use of a similar milieu as protagonist that later fuses in *Paterson, Book I* into a powerful criticism of our social morality. In the earlier poem the desolate finality of the short "No one" and its repetition in the long last line in terms of a frightening detail from the modern world—a driverless car—heightens the solitariness of Elsie's (and everybody's) situation, while at the same time it suggests the cause of her plight. I should say that this poem represents a didactic impulse of a high order. But it is so deficient in the element of rhetoric which most of us have come to expect in didactic poetry that the finesse of the moral judgment may escape some readers. For, confused by bad nineteenth-century models, we have come to identify the hortatory with the didactic to the detriment of both qualities in modern poetry.

In LX, a little masterpiece of its kind, we again see this subtle mode of social evaluation. The poem is about the time of year when boys fifteen and seventeen, "drivers for grocers or taxi-drivers" . . . "Wear two-horned lilac blossoms in their caps—or over one ear." They are

> Dirty satyrs, it is
> vulgarity raised to the last power.

But there is no condemnation in this exact, realistic judgment, merely a humorous tolerance based on a secret recognition of the elemental and regenerative forces in nature for which the boys act:

They stand in the doorways
on the business streets with a sneer
on their faces

adorned with blossoms

Out of their sweet heads
dark kisses—rough faces

. . . .

The Descent of Winter (1927) seems, as the title hints,
a temporarily barren stretch in Williams' development.
While the poems are technically as excellent as those in
Spring and All, there appears to be a casting about for
subject matter and meaning. The very method of organization suggests that the poems were written as notations,
as jottings in a diary or journal. There is a spurious unity
given by entry dates above each poem. The dates com-
mence at the end of September and end with December
15th, thus documenting the title. In the *CP* Williams includes only eight poems, the series ceasing at 11/28. The
idea seems to be to record the emotional biography of the
poet through presenting a more or less sustained mood,
a nucleus of experience grouped around a season, a season
which is also a season of the soul. The themes repeat
Williams' earlier interests. The problem of age ("What
chance have the old?"), the awareness of poverty as "one
with the meanness of love," the recording of the surfaces
of industrial society—freight cars, popular tunes, electric
signboards of young men in running pants "with ecstatic,
aesthetic faces" make up the bulk of the notations. There
is a note of disturbed questioning of the poet's own powers,
as in "9/30":

> This is the sadness of the sea—
> waves like words, all broken—
> a sameness of lifting and falling mood.

In the entry for 11/28 this is cancelled by an arrogant assertion of belief in his election of value:

> I make really very little money.
> What of it?
> I prefer the grass with the rain on it
> the short grass before my headlights
>
> when I am turning the car—
> a degenerate trait, no doubt.
> It would ruin England.

The entry for 11/2, the only one dignified by a title, is "A Morning Imagination of Russia" and the most ambitious poem in *The Descent of Winter*. It relates the thoughts of a Russian who is able to make comparisons between the old world of cities and the new world which was "the very old past . . . refound/redirected . . ." This man is capable, unlike his latter-day descendants, of humility and doubt as to the wisdom of his own commitments: "He felt/uncertain many days. But all were uncertain/together and he must weigh for them out/of himself."

> We have cut out the cancer but
> who knows? perhaps the patient will die

Still, the affirmative quality of the operation is stressed at the very end in Williams' favorite vocabulary of that period: ". . . We have paid heavily. But we/have gotten —touch." This was what Williams had urged as editor of *Contact*, what he was writing about in letters to his friends

59

at this time, and what was already in a sense the underlying emotional orientation of much of his poetry. Togetherness, contact, touch, these were goals both for society and art in a world that seemed tragically "cut from touch." The poem is more interesting for its foreshadowing of Williams' later political interests than as an achievement in itself. We can see the motivation for some of the hazardous political excursions Williams was to make in the future along with many of his fellow poets, here and abroad.

The years 1923–27, then, as reflected in *The Descent of Winter* seem to have been a stalemate in Williams' otherwise clear line of progress. There is throughout a barren attachment to sterile still-life pictograms, as in the first poem "9/29," which suggests that Williams was making a revision of his accomplishment and had not yet sifted out what he wished to keep.

. . . .

When, in 1934, Williams' *Collected Poems* came out under the aegis of the Objectivist Press of which he had been one of the co-founders, and in whose previous publication, an *Objectivist Anthology,* he had already appeared, the critical reaction to this selection of work from 1921–31 together with a few poems from the 'teens, was moulded by Wallace Stevens' introduction to the volume. Stevens' brisk comments, many of them sound enough, but none of them really exhaustive of Williams' quality or achievement, today still form the stock-pile of the academic understanding of Williams' work.

The main direction of Stevens' friendly preface was that

THE POEMS

Williams by "rejecting the accepted sense of things" was substituting a romanticism of his own. Inherent in this romanticism is a sentimental vein which, in fact, is "the reaction from sentiment." The anti-poetic is the cure for the spirit to the sentimental side of Williams. "Something of the unreal is necessary to fecundate the real; something of the sentimental is necessary to fecundate the anti-poetic. Williams, by nature is more of a realist than is commonly true in the case of a poet." But Stevens is careful to add: "All poets are, to some extent, romantic poets." He concludes by listing "Some veritable additions to the corpus of poetry" made by Williams: his special use of the anti-poetic, the ambiguity produced by bareness, the implied image as an addition to Imagism, as a phase of realism, and his exquisite writing about flowers.

But where Stevens had qualified his application of the term "romantic," like other convenient labels it stuck —and without the qualification. Over a decade later in "Rubbings of Reality," a tribute to Williams, Stevens could redefine his work in such a way as to implicitly negate the "romantic" tag. The need to get to the bottom of the disintegration of the modern world, said Stevens is not emotional: "It springs from the belief that we have only our intelligence on which to rely . . . If we could suddenly remake the world on the basis of our own intelligence, see it clearly and represent it without faintness or obscurity, Williams' poems would have a place there." [7] It is clear, then, that the tag of "romantic" on Williams is no more useful than on D. H. Lawrence or W. B. Yeats. All

[7] *Briarcliff Quarterly,* October 1946.

three, it might be pointed out, are similarly "anti-intellec-
tual," but at least one is highly traditional and "literary"
in his orientation (the early and middle Yeats). Yeats's
mysticism is the polar antithesis of Williams' "realism,"
while at the same time, as we have seen, it is possible for a
perceptive critic like Yvor Winters to classify Williams
simultaneously as a primitive and a traditionalist. T. S.
Eliot, taking his legislative stand with classicism, in practice is often romantic. The point to all this is that we never
get insight into the specific quality of a given poem if we
approach it by tabloid antitheses.

I should prefer, then, to forget the generalizations of
Stevens' preface when looking at the *Collected Poems* and
to remember only the particular qualities he assigns as
Williams' contribution. The *Collected Poems* sum up
the distinctive individual features in Williams' sensibility
up to 1934, and at the same time consolidate on a richer
level of integration the gains of his early Imagist, free-
verse and Objectivist disciplines. While some of the best
poems rely on a heightened precision of observation, as,
for example, in "The House," "In the 'Sconset Bus," "The
Red Lily," "Nantucket" and "On Gay Wallpaper," almost all of them add another dimension of perception to
the almost purely pictorial scale of academic Imagism.

"The House," one of those fresh studies in a genre
in which Williams had by now come to excel—the tidy
milieu of domesticity—shows us implications attired in
a clean, homely speech. It is a speech which builds up
both the nuances of affection and that communion of
shared struggle and achievement in marriage which is,

perhaps, its most typical but uncelebrated good. A comparison of the printed version with an early draft in the U.B. Collection is instructive.

As might be expected from Williams' usual emphasis on economy, bareness, whittling down, his procedure is to suppress more and more of the detail. In the earlier draft (I have no way of determining whether it is the first) the maid's name "Lucy" is given, rowels newly painted are mentioned in the description of the stairs, the bathroom is included in the list of domestic accoutrements awaiting the lady of the house, and she is told she will not have to live in one hotel room any longer (Williams' wife, Floss, was then travelling in Europe). To suppress Lucy is wise; she is not essential to the story. The emphasis is more properly left with the wife, the "you" of the poem, who, after all, is the central personage of the poem and is herself unnamed. It is enough to know that the front stairs have been freshly painted, "white tiers/and the treads mahogany"; we do not need to know about the rowels—they add nothing to the structural features of the stairs which are composed for us in the lines above. The suppression of the bathroom requires no comment. As for the deletion of the lines about the hotel room, they were merely an explanatory note on the homecoming which we do not need to appreciate its joyousness.

There is another category of change in the suppression of emotive words: For example, "remember how we stood here and wondered/with the hogshead/of crockery/in one eccentric center" becomes simply:

> This is the front room
> where we stood penniless
> by the hogshead of crockery.

The omission of "and wondered" juxtaposes the concrete word "penniless" (calling up the image of the young couple facing the blankness of the future) with the fresh, domestic detail of the "hogshead of crockery" (evoking the quality of anticipation of a new life in a new home); the two together combine into a delicate mood of pathos and nostalgia. There is something pathetic about young, poverty-stricken marriage, but there is also something adventurous and exciting which perhaps the older couple would wish to recapture. This backward glance together with the present joy in renewal (that is, of the meaning of *home*) make up the emotional texture of the poem.

Another class of changes consists in the stressing, by repetition, of key words like "awaits" and "please." The early draft has "Come walk up/the stairs to the bedroom/ your bedroom/awaits/the chiffonier waits/", while the final version reads:

> Come upstairs
> to the bedroom—
> Your bed awaits you
> The chiffonier waits
>
> the whole house
> is waiting—for you

The repetitive "waits" and the accented "waiting" suggests a quality of intimate relationship between a house and the personalities of the people who live in it which the early draft does not. The completion of the short-lined quatrain with

> to walk in at your pleasure—
> It is yours.

implies a gracious, open-handed generosity of giving (all the inanimate objects, the whole house, in fact, are waiting for the mistress to take possession) which is the courtesy of love, no less when it is hot-water heaters and gas-stoves we are giving than when it was pomegranates and pearls. The word "pleasure" in the next to the last line as it grows out of and generalizes the earlier "to please you" of stanza 3 and the "as you please" of stanza 1 is a lucid demonstration of the way this homely progression of details spreads out from a simple factual center and glows into an almost ritual celebration of domesticity. "It is yours" serves as summary, climax and final presentation of the gift of love which the house has come to be.

Thus, it can be seen that Williams may start with a modest experience (even his epic *Paterson* begins with the one, rather than the many, with the immediate rather than the remote) but what becomes of this "innocence" along the way is an entirely different matter. Mr. Parker Tyler has analyzed this process in an ingenious way in the seemingly "primitive" "This is Just to Say," a note written by the poet to his wife apologizing for the fact that he has eaten the plums she had put in the icebox for breakfast. "The irony of this poem," writes Mr. Tyler, "was that precisely that which preserved them (the plums) and increased the deliciousness of their perfection (the refrigeration) contained in its essence the sensuous quality most closely associated with death; coldness. So the plums' death (or formal disappearance and disintegration) was symbolically anticipated in the charm of their living flesh. This is, I believe, the exact pathos of this brief poem . . ." [8]

The range of implication is similarly deepened in another group in the *Collected Poems* by extracting fresh meanings from more traditional symbols. One could compare how Williams utilizes the bull-procreation connection in "The Bull," for example, with the way Yeats has reexamined the mortal-god intercourse myths in "Leda and the Swan." In "The Bull" which Wallace Stevens lumps together with "The Cod Head" as "pure sentimentalization" (but of a sort which he apparently approves), the bull is described, godlike in captivity, living alone, while the sun,

> Olympian commentary on
> the bright passage of days.
> . . .
>
> smooths his lacquer
> through
> the glossy pinetrees
>
> his substance hard
> as ivory or glass—
> through which the wind
> yet plays—

Like the "Olympian" sun the bull is a principle of power. But as the wind can play through the hard substance (light) of the sun, so too the bull is not a principle *in vacuo*. For while the physical qualities stressed in the

[8] *Briarcliff Quarterly*, October 1946.

bull, for example "half-closed eyes," etc., are precisely those which emphasize his seeming self-sufficiency, his actual dependence for continuity on other forces in the physical universe is arrived at by a subtle addition:

> Milkless
> he nods
> the hair between his horns
> and eyes matted
> with hyacinthine curls

It is the isolation of the single word "Milkless" which performs for us the whole act of judgment Williams would have us make of the bull. Without a complementary generative principle, the bull's fecundating powers are sterile, "milkless." [9] This is an oblique way of emphasizing the interdependence of processes in the physical universe. Williams with his scientific realism could never, like D. H. Lawrence isolate one symbol—the serpent—let us say, and let it carry *all* the generative weight of the universe. This, it seems to me, is the opposite of sentiment. Williams builds up an exact, almost traditional picture of the bull,

[9] There is a fascinating prose parallel to this poem in the recent "Letter to an Australian Editor." Williams opposes the "classic" view that "mind . . . fertilizes mind . . . without female . . . bred androgynetically." Against this view he proposes "another literary source continuing the greatness of the past which does not develop androgynetically from the past itself, mind to mind, but from the present, from the hurley burley of political encounters which determine or may determine it, direct.

A man may live for a time on a gathered hoard of skills, granted, but if he lives his meat will run out unless replenished about him. He will continue to produce only if his attachments to society continue adequate. If a man in his fatuous dreams cuts himself off from that supplying female, he dries up his sources . . ." *Briarcliff Quarterly,* No. 11, October 1946.

only to rescue it from the danger of "poetic" *stylization* by the significant qualification I have discussed.

In "The Winds," a short, powerful and ironic poem, Williams uses the cleansing violence of the winds very much as St.-John Perse was to use rain symbolism in his long poem "The Rains" fifteen years later. The title functioning (as in many of Williams' poems of this period) as first line is particularly ingenious here because "winds" is the grammatical subject of all the verbs in the poem and the actual subject-matter (symbolically) of the whole poem as well. By a mounting progression of detail, the winds blowing the bark from the trees, the soil from the field, the hair from the heads of girls, the cross from the church, etc., we finally arrive at:

> . . . . crusts
> from scabby eyes, scales from
> the mind and husbands from wives

This is certainly a clean sweep! It is useful to notice how quiet is the irony of the final "husbands from wives" left hanging in the path of a renewing destruction without even an anchoring punctuation mark as solace.

A large number of poems in the *Collected Poems* springs from an examination of the facts of the modern world, or those historical facts which inhabit and qualify the present. The tone is often satiric, with a finer rapier-thrust of implication than in Williams' earlier poems in this style. "The Sea-Elephant" (displayed in a circus side-show), might be counter-posed to "The Bull" as the modern, "anti-poetic" types of Eros. The unnamed person who says in a practical voice "They/ought/to put it back where/it came from," is making precisely the right comment on the dislocated appetite which "love" has become in the modern world, as dislocated as seems the huge appetite of the sea-monster when he is out of his proper element.[10]

The other side of the coin of appetite which the sea-elephant represents is drawn in a poem about a dead man, its implications universalized by the title, "Death." It is a poem which stems from the same acceptance of death as the term of all being, as had Williams' earlier "Total Destruction" but it extends the implications. For now death is equated with the negation of love; the negation of love is "a mockery" to the living. It is for this reason that death, the negative pole of experience, is shameful:

> he's dead
> the old bastard—
> He's a bastard because
>
> there's nothing
> legitimate in him any
> more

---

[10] Although, like many poets, Williams does not seem to be the best reader of his own poems, his reading of this one is revealing. His half-playful, half-agonized reading of the monster's plea:

> Blouaugh! (feed
> me) my flesh is riven—
> . . .
>
> contort yourselves
> But I am love. I am
> from the sea—

customarily emphasizes "(*feed* me)."

This poem, while containing many powerful passages, I do not consider entirely successful. The last three lines beginning ". . . and spring . . ." are too obvious in their appeal to authority as a satiric counterpoint to the sea-monster's natural appetite.

he's dead
He's sick dead

he's
a godforsaken curio
without
any breath in it

He's nothing at all
  he's dead
. . . .

just bury it
and hide its face—
for shame

   The most shameful thing about death, all kinds of death, both living death and dead death, is that "love cannot touch" it. The short, stabbing brutality of the lines, the repetition of the key word "dead" with twists of accent like "He's sick dead"; the harsh, almost profane tone of rejection in the epithets applied to the man (note the ironic play of wit in the progression from "the old bastard" to the explanation of the corpse's bastardy by the etymologically literal but poignant information that he's a bastard because "there's nothing/legitimate in him any/more"). Williams' idea of the utter degradation of non-being (here and elsewhere equated with physical death) as being "cut from touch," that is to say, love, is similar to e. e. cummings' concept of "un" (not) which for him becomes the prefix most evocative of human degradation. They are contemporaries, and the possible influence of one upon the other (they admire each other's work) is difficult to unravel. "Death" is a good illustration of the way in which the use of anti-poetic detail can be made to spread out into affirmative meanings. That is to say, the recognition of anti-poetic detail does not, as Matthew Arnold thought of Whitman, commit one to nihilism. It may instead prelude a thoroughly non-materialistic, affirmative humanism, even when, as with Williams and cummings, suggesting pagan rather than Christian views of mortality.

But in "The Trees" the affirmation of love is openly loosed from any moorings it may have in classical myth, and the poet seeks to put it (and myth) back where it came from—in man:

> There were never satyrs
> never maenads
> never eagle-headed gods—
> These were men
> from whose hands sprung
> love
> bursting the wood—
>
> Trees their companions
> . . . . .

And in "Rain," a beautiful love lyric which consists of a tautly sustained metaphor, beginning,

> As the rain falls
> so does
>   your love
>
> bathe every
>   open
> Object of the world—

the rain is contrasted with "the priceless dry-rooms/of/illicit/loves," the all-renewing rain in which

71

The trees
are become
beasts fresh risen
from
        the sea—
water

trickles
from the crevices of
their hides—

But the poet spends his life "to keep out love" and while the rain, "a kind physician," makes new organisms come "into form from its/liquid/clearness," there is the nonmaterial self-containedness, the autotelic nature of "love" to be distinguished from the purely physical renewal of nature by the rain: For love is a human act of creation,

        and nothing
    comes of it but love

This, and other love poems (see especially my discussion of "Perpetuum Mobile") would seem to give the lie to Williams' "naturalism." Always, the genesis of this "unworldly" love is in ". . . men, from whose hands sprung/ love." This wise ordering measures the gulf between Williams' essentially rational humanism and D. H. Lawrence's mystical sexual monism.

The knife of the times begins to cut in more deeply in *Collected Poems,* and sometimes it elicits a wry, nostalgic, tongue-in-cheek humor as in "Hemmed in Males" which laments the plight of the American male when the Volstead Act closed the saloons with no place left to go "except home." This poem is instructive for showing Williams' use of American idiom without a resort to jargon or slang, but with a sound reliance on the *structure* of speech patterns to clarify the locale. "It is a Living Coral" satirizes in montage fashion the "facts" of American history, while "This Florida: 1924" shows Williams' nose (the "strong-ridged" one he had addressed years before in "Smell" with "Must you taste everything?") for pretense and fake in social façades. It is in this poem, incidentally, that there occurs one of Williams' many recantations of any allegiance he might still be thought to hold to Imagism:

> And we thought to escape rime
> by imitation of the senseless
> unarrangement of wild things—

"Down-town" is a whimsical account of the persistence of fancy in an age of T-beams and wire cables when a boy with a rose "under the lintel of his cap" will stand to have his picture taken on the butt of a girder with the city a mile down, wearing a "rose-petal" smile, and stirring a thought of Indians on chestnut branches. The closing line of this poem "to end 'walking on the air,' " shows Williams employing the device of quotation which Marianne Moore has made a particular trademark.

The implied antithesis of "Down-town" (really a snapshot composition) is dynamized into a little playlet in "The Jungle," a sophisticated paring down of the Browning monologue structure which Pound, Eliot and Williams had all employed in their early work. We learn that the jungle is not "the still weight of the trees, the breathless interior of the wood," the vines, flies, reptiles, monkeys, etc.

73

> but
> a girl waiting
> shy, brown, soft-eyed—
> to guide you
>   Upstairs, sir . . .

All the copy-book rules for portraiture are broken in this poem. The true subject is the jungle, that is to say, the jungle of the brown girl's personality. But we arrive at this negatively by hearing all the things a "jungle" (at a literal level of implication) is not. The interesting connection between these two kinds of jungles is that some of the meanings denied to the first one, carry over by means of technical brilliance to the "jungle" character of the girl. For example, the "breathless interior" of the wood, "the still weight of the trees" are implicit in the breathless, still "waiting" of the girl, are stressed, in fact, by the sibilant mysteriousness of the lines: "shy, brown, soft-eyed . . . Upstairs, sir," as well as by the weak feminine end-syllable of the last line. We reach fresh definition of a true jungle quality by delineation of the girl against a conventional "jungle" back-drop.

In "April," an ambitious but, on the whole, unsuccessful effort, Williams' swift, pictogrammic flashes of modern experience in terms of signs, menus, advertisements, etc., are marshalled into a motion-picture cavalcade of the commonplace daily events which weave the texture of our living. The best features of these rather thinly connected passages are in the small portraits of special modern types reported either in third person narrative or in the betraying cadences of their own speech. There is the crisp, vivid, "Moral" (a recurrent sign or device—like "Excelsior!") of

> the redhead sat
> in bed with her legs
> crossed and talked
> rough stuff

There is the malicious neuroticism of modern love in

> You would "kill me with kindness"
> I love you too, but I love you
> *too—*

And there is the trig summary of this attempt to capture "The clatter and true sound/of verse" in the closing lines where we are seen to recognize "the shapes of things":

> only in the white heat of
> understanding, when a flame
> runs through the gap made
> by learning . . .

After this somewhat uneasy attempt at literal visual signification in "April," Williams allowed the total metrical pattern to carry whatever visual representation the poem entailed.

. . . .

By 1935, when *An Early Martyr* appeared, the economic and social pressures on writers, as on other Americans, were operating to move them in the direction of "class consciousness." But the decade of "social" poetry precipitated by the fact of the economic holocaust of the whole Western world, eventually set up a vortex, secondary to its central causation, which was meretricious and fashionable. Many "innocent" writers were sucked into this vortex. To be "socially conscious" was as much a categorical imperative for many poets of the '30's as to be "Ivory Tower" in the '90's. An unhealthy and shallow mass conversion of this kind threw up many strange bedfellows among the poets as well as among those they were trying to emulate. But, it must be emphasized that Williams, for all his ill-advised and often brash polemical writing during this period, never directly affiliated himself with any party or programmatic politico-literary group. The fact that various groups tried to claim him for their own is an entirely distinct matter and if a "proletarian" critic wishes to see "The Yachts" (which I shall discuss later) as representing the struggle between the privileged class and the laboring class in which "The yachts, which symbolize the privileged class, as they skim over inland waters, are contrasted with the biggest hulls—the underprivileged, or the laboring class, exposed to the cruel buffetings of the heavy seas . . ." what is a defenseless poet to do about it?

It would be just as misleading, on the other hand, to judge Williams' poems of this period by the tenets of Objectivism as they were somewhat cryptically enunciated by the ideological spokesman of the group, Louis Zukofsky. While there was mention of objectivists, and objectification, (a poem as objectification is successful if it is words resolved into a structure "to which the mind does not wish to add.") Objectivism, as a *principle* of writing, was explicated largely through pointing to the work of poets like Basil Bunting, John Wheelwright, Zukofsky or Williams himself. Williams when later asked to define Objectivism by an under-graduate group at Dartmouth said somewhat paradoxically that while there was no "objectivist" poetry, "Objectivism has to do with the whole poem—the structure of the poem as a metrical invention—a complete objective significance uniquely in itself above any partial image which it may contain."

For Williams a program, as we have seen in his relatively speedy rejection of Imagism, is merely a pole toward which his energies for a while may tend. His habit is first to devalue the fixed exchange put on any slogan whether in art or politics. Temperamentally, Williams could never submit to a received discipline whether of last month's literary manifesto or yesterday's party caucus. In the twenties he had written: "One must continually break down what one has accomplished. One must come out clean. One is not tricked or beaten into acquiescence except by physical decay."

In *An Early Martyr,* the title poem is appreciably the weakest, for Williams makes too obvious concessions to a conventional economic determinism when explaining the behavior of the young thief who sent postcards to the police to come and arrest him. He judges the young man's pilfering as

> Signalizing
> the romantic period
> Of a revolt

Williams himself romanticizes the consequences of the young man's romanticism when he exhorts us not to give up

77

> to such bought
> Courts as he thought
> to trust but they
> Double-crossed him

The courts may be "bought," but this instance of their functioning is not especially persuasive of that conclusion.

Making a swift comeback from this failure of judgment, Williams in the tough and witty "A Poem for Norman Macleod" advises the younger poet who was then sloughing off his own past "proletarian" encumbrances to remember that:

> The revolution
> is accomplished
> noble has been
> changed to no bull.

The pun is here legitimate. Williams puns in order to translate a fashionable "noble" value as it connected with a then-accepted fashion, "the revolution," into a fresh equation. Let's not be metaphysical about the sanctions the revolution casts upon art; let us merely be honest, he urges, in the crisp imagery of Chief One Horn's advice to the prospector as he gashed a balsam and gathered the gum:

> it did the trick

> You can do lots
> if you know
> what's around you
> No bull

THE POEMS

Begin with the homely, familiar therapy that lies in a thorough understanding of the world about you, a world which if you "know" it (for Williams, "know," in this sense, always means "to raise to the imagination") you can do lots with. That is the sense, Williams is saying, in which an artist accomplishes revolutions. Williams' advice is, considering the context of the times, radical, as radical as the gashing of the balsam tree by the medicine man.

In the tender "The Dead Baby," in the closely drawn Breughel-like figure of the young bare-headed woman in "Proletarian Portrait," in the compassionate, involuntary contrast of the desiccated old woman and the ripe plums of "To a Poor Old Woman," and in the fidelity to fact and speech of "Sunday," Williams showed what one could do if one knew what was about him. But it is in the more ambitious "The Raper from Passenack," that Williams makes a powerful indictment of the world about him. Here he works again in that nexus of working-class, suburban brutality which he had illuminated in "To Elsie." The quality of the raper's speech, as well as that of his victim's, is an oblique illumination of the cruel impersonality and primitive superstitiousness of the modern industrial world on whose dingy peripheries they live. The wry understatement of the opening lines (here again the title functioning as first line) sets the tone for the whole sordid American tragedy:

THE RAPER FROM PASSENACK

was very kind. When she regained
her wits, he said, It's all right, Kid,
I took care of you.

79

What a mess she was in. Then he added
You'll never forget me now.
And drove her home.

. . . .

It is to be noted that Williams has isolated, in a specially dramatized framework, to be sure, the underlying neuroticism of modern sexual behavior. The raper does not rape from lust for pleasure, like Tarquin, or for generative fulfillment of his own nature like the swan in the Greek myth, but almost without emotion at all, unless from the pathetic desire to be recognized. The fact that the raper wants to be remembered, that is to say, seeks to leave some evidence of his existence in the consciousness of another person is a bitter consequence to the deprivation of adequate proofs of the individual's reality which occur in an impersonal, power-narcotized society. But Williams does not try to assign responsibility for this failure. I have drawn the social implications implicit in the poem. Williams merely presents the individual case history, clinically, and without comment.

Still, in the compassionate and lyrical absolution of "The Catholic Bells," reminiscent in structure of the cumulative progression of "The Winds," and foreshadowing the more ambitious "The Pink Church," Williams impartially rings down the benediction of a Sunday peace on all the persons of this ugly suburban world, upon the leaves, the flowers, the new baby, "the parrot under its hood/jealous of the child," and "old age which adds/as it/takes away,"

. . . O Bells
ring for the ringing!

THE POEMS

The cumulative effect of the bell-metaphor is to resolve human frailty and imperfection into the joyous abandon of forgiveness for its own sake ("ring for the ringing!").

"The Yachts," which I have mentioned in another connection, is the most ambitious undertaking in *An Early Martyr* and a departure from Williams' former practice. Beginning, as always, with the simple physical data—in this instance, the yachts—Williams evokes a vivacious image of their brilliant, youthful beauty. But suddenly the physical referents are expanded into universals more overtly than had been Williams' earlier custom when the reader had been given the responsibility for making the concrete particulars yield the universals—of, so to speak, extracting the essence from the vial. Here, in the sixth of eleven unusually long-lined stanzas, their dominantly hexametric cast suggesting the sinuous movements of the yachts, the "youthful" kinesis of the yachts is directly equated with the rarity of

> . . . the light of a happy eye, live with the grace
> of all that in the mind is feckless, free and
> naturally to be desired . . .

". . . feckless, free and naturally to be desired," that, for once, we are *told* is the significance of the yacht as symbol and we think that this summarizes the thematic intention. But suddenly, by pursuing the implications of the metaphor, the symbolism begins to reshape itself, to suggest new concretions of meaning.

Technically, the transition is excellently managed. Immediately after "desired" there is a double caesura and even the sea's threat against the crisp vessels "fails completely." But then the winds come and the yachts are off, slipping through the waves which strike at them because they are "too well-made." Without preparation, but with the curious naturalness and inevitability of a dream, the three concluding stanzas show the yachts, in a stunning revelation of their total nature, as recklessly cruel and destructive in their beautiful independence:

> Arms with hands grasping seek to clutch at the prows.
> Bodies thrown recklessly in the way are cut aside.
> It is a sea of faces about them in agony, in despair
>
> until the horror of the race dawns staggering the mind,
> the whole sea become an entanglement of watery bodies
> lost to the world bearing what they cannot hold. Broken,
>
> beaten, desolate, reaching from the dead to be taken up
> they cry out, failing, failing! their cries rising
> in waves still as the skillful yachts pass over.

Whose arms? The arms are the arms of those who seek to possess or adjoin themselves to that which "in the mind is feckless, free and naturally to be desired." Now we understand the "horror" of the race: the human contender cannot keep pace with or merge into the beautiful, self-contained dynamism of the ideal. And, ruthlessly, magnificent, relentless machines, "the skillful yachts pass over." The referents of the yacht-race metaphor have expanded into both a moral allegory and a judgment on the nature of the ideal. One can take the poem either at the level of aesthetic or of philosophical speculation. One can see it as a contest between beauty and desire, between the contradictions set up by human imperfection and the

THE POEMS

cruel elusiveness of the "ideal" which as Yeats also knew,
man "lock, stock and barrel, made with his bitter heart."

Williams' usual interest in the data of the natural universe seems in *An Early Martyr* subordinate to his ethical
and social speculations. Of the two or three poems dealing
with purely "natural" phenomena, however, at least one,
"The Locust Tree in Flower," is a small tour de force of
Williams' early Imagist method, now tightened by a more
sophisticated syntax and compelled by a purer lyric intention.

Among
of
green

stiff
old
bright

broken
branch
come

white
sweet
May

again

It will be remarked at once that each line except the
first, the seventh and the last are single-stressed and monosyllabic. Thus, the swift comet-like structure of the poem
is given a spinal support or brace at the beginning, middle
and end. Also, the similarity in stress pattern of the first

and last lines creates a circular union of the total cadence. I conceive of the poem as representing a single speech unit, with a brief caesura after "come."

.   .   .   .

In *Adam and Eve and The City* (1936), we find Williams turning his eye more and more inward. There are the familiar small, crisp still-lives of man, beast and flower, but the important poems continue an investigation of inner experience. The result is a more subjective tone than we had come to associate with him. But "subjectivity" in poetry is a relative state rather than the representation of a polar antithesis between it and "objectivity."

The poems are uniformly longer, some, in fact, being as long as the "longer poems" which Williams has grouped separately in his *CCP*. Of the long poems in *Adam and Eve and The City*, "Perpetuum Mobile" is both the most adventurous and the most successful. Indeed, it is one of Williams' most hauntingly lovely pieces. It has apparently haunted the poet, too, for we find him using it almost ten years later as a leitmotif in his play *A Dream of Love*, a title which is another reflection of the poem. Using a stabbing, predominantly two-stressed line, the curious broken rhythm suggests the searching desire of love which is its central theme. The poem begins with the personal roots of the subject in the poet's experience. Inevitably, and by the very nature of love's compulsion, it broadens into an evaluation of "love" and "desire" as universals; universals, but not, it should be emphasized, as abstractions. The typographical placement of the subtitle "The City" suggests that the city can be thought of

84

THE POEMS

as background to the dream as well as the all-containing, glittering symbolic goal toward which love strives. The poem begins:

        —a dream
    we dreamed
        each
    separately
        we two

    of love
        and of
    desire—

    that fused
    in the night—

    in the distance
        over
    the meadows
        by day
    impossible—
        The city
    disappeared
        when
    we arrived—

        A dream
    a little false
    toward which
        now
    we stand
        and stare
    transfixed—

It is the separateness of the dream which makes fusion possible *only* at night, and "by day impossible," for night is the time of dream and illusion and thus confers an ambiguity on such experience, which, nevertheless, does not lessen its significance in our lives.

> a dream
>   toward which
> we love—
> at night
>   more
> than a little false—

The paradox of love's compulsion ("there is no end/to desire—") is that it *is* a dream, more than a little false, "a dream of love" toward which we love, a dream, moreover, we have each made for ourselves "separately." This is somewhat the same paradox Shakespeare considered in *A Midsummer Night's Dream* (another dream of love) as well as, in a more generally philosophic vein, in *The Tempest*. The heavenly city disappears when we arrive, and "reality" (equated with "day") catches up with us again:

> We have bred
> We have dug
> we have figured up
> our costs
> we have bought
> an old rug
> We batter at our
> unsatisfactory
>   brilliance

The poet urges us to break through the mold of custom and "go there," only to echo himself with a disenchanted "in vain!" There are presented various examples of love's magnetic dynamism. We see the guards who have been protecting the armored truck of money *themselves* holding up the bank. "For love!"; we get a sordid glimpse of whorishness for love; the suicides "their eyes blown out," for love; the rich "Guzzling the cream food" while in the sub-cellar is "the foulest sink in the world!" Suddenly the poet cries "No end—"; there is no end to the ways in which the dream can be perceived and the ways in which, like a polar magnet, it moves men to action, for "There is no end/to desire—." The City is then asked to bring silence to the dream (the City is not only the heavenly city of love, but also the real city which encompasses this variegated landscape of aspiration and despair). Now it is the "Tearful city" which even as we look at it on a summer's day loses its hard, definite outlines and dwindles "in a wall of rain—." The poet bids farewell to it, the notes of his leavetaking in the last line blending subtly with the melancholy of the "wall of rain" into which the city (the "real" city; the heavenly city of love) has dwindled.

In "St. Francis Einstein of the Daffodil," a poem with at least one fine stanza ("O Samos, Samos/dead and buried . . ."), but the center of which I cannot discover, we find Williams experimenting with the use of refrain which he had employed subtly in "Perpetuum Mobile" to ring in the melancholy, eternizing note of recurrence. Similarly, in "Eve," a companion piece to the successful "Adam," there is a consistent use of repetitive and parenthesized refrain. It is here employed for irony.

"Eve," beginning

> Pardon my injuries
> now that you are old

is a terrifying but poignant summary of the meaning of old age. It is as if all the preliminary studies of old age which Williams had made were here, in his own approaching old age, fused into an agonized perception of its significance, derived from the knowledge of one's own sources, one's parents ("Adam" and "Eve"). The perception, put in over-simple terms, is similar to Yeats's persistent and wracking judgment on his own old age: the will, the desire, the imagination persisting without the capacity to perform. The old woman in "Eve" cannot "hold a knife to cut the meat" but the same fingers

> in a hypnotic ecstasy
> can so wrench a hand held out
> to you that our bones
> crack under the unwonted pressure—

The vision is so precise it is almost cruel. The cruelty is relieved by the poet's guilt for the accuracy of his insight. His expiation benefits the poem.

.   .   .   .

In "Recent Verse (1938)," the penultimate section in *CCP* representing the work of Williams' mid-fifties, one senses an effort to throw off the introspective habit so eloquently confessed in *Adam and Eve and The City* two years before and to lose and thus find the "self" again in a vision closer to the external configurations of society. There is a resultant colloquial veracity in the social types distinguished in "At the Bar: from 'Paterson,'" and in other sketches for the projected Paterson sequence. Two of these short poems will point up Williams' method in

THE POEMS

this genre. One, "At the Bar," relies on the colorful metaphor of a slang derived from the electric age:

> Hi, open up a dozen.
>
> Wha'cha trying to do—
> charge ya batteries?
>
> Make it two.
>   Easy girl!
> You'll blow a fuse if
> ya keep that up.

The fact that this breezy accuracy (the talk creating the saloon setting, the customer, and the barmaid addressed as well) is not so easy to do as its off-handedness would suggest, is evidenced by the three extant MS versions in the U.B. Collection.

In "To Greet A Letter Carrier" one sees that Williams is not seduced by the topical vivacity of slang but is interested in the structure of American speech cadences:

> Why'n't you bring me
> a good letter? One with
> lots of money in it.
> I could make use of that.
> Atta boy! Atta boy!

In a talk to Dartmouth students, Williams recommended Mencken's 3rd edition of *The American Language* as a text and proceeded to define his interest in language:

. . . I believe all art begins in the local and must begin there since only then will the senses find their material. Our own language is the beginning of that which makes and will continue to make an American poetry distinctive—

As a consequence in some of my work all I have to do is to transcribe the language when hot and feelingly spoken. For when it is charged with emotion it has a tendency to be rhythmic, lowdown, inherent in the place where it is being used. And that is, to me, the origin of form, the origin of measure. The rhythmic beat of charged language.

Williams modestly did not add that the transcribing was the making of the poem.

Williams' interest in the precise record of American speech may seem like a naturalist's myopia to the same critics who can, for example, appreciate Proust's careful fidelity in transcribing the Breton patois of Françoise. The interest which in Williams may be deemed "narrow" or "parochial," in Proust, removed as he is by another language and by the even greater sanctification of death, we recognize more truly for what it is: an interest in language for its own sake, as an area of asthetic experience, and also for its rich capacity to elucidate the structure of personality, class, milieu, and an age. More particularly, for Williams spoken language is the norm from which poetic measure derives and from which it should seek its perpetual refreshment.

Just as "low-down" language seemed to Williams' ears to have a charged quality of rhythm which might be elevated into a metric, so his delighted response to the visual anarchy of low-down districts provides him with an aesthetic of poverty. In a poem like "The Poor" Williams' enjoyment of "the anarchy of poverty" is not a romanticizing of its picturesqueness but a sharp comment on its dynamics,

> the dress of the children
> reflecting every stage and
> custom of necessity.

It is precisely because Williams *sees* the social concomitants of poverty that he is yet able to take joy in its implicit non-conformity, its "anarchy."

Throughout "Recent Verse" there is a heavier reliance on titles which serve as first lines of poems. "The Sun," "A Bastard Peace," "Middle," and "These" are examples.

> THESE
> when nature in its barrenness
> are the desolate dark weeks
> equals the stupidity of man

deals with the poet's despair among "the flashes and booms of war," a despair which leads him to a consideration of death: "the people gone that we love,/the beds lying empty . . ." There is an ironic resignation accompanied by an undertone of incredulity:

> In this mine they come to dig—all.
> Is this the counter-foil to sweetest
>
> music? The source of poetry that
> seeing the clock stopped, says
> The clock has stopped
>
> That ticked yesterday so well?
> and hears the sound of lakewater
> splashing—that is now stone.

The mention of war in "These," the title "A Bastard Peace," and the weary, frustrated mood of "Middle" with children "giving lustily to the memory/of our war dead," all reflect a consciousness of the imminence of war. It is interesting to notice that as with Eliot and Joyce the first World War, as brute event, made little impact on Williams' work. It was only after the war that Eliot wrote *The Waste Land* as a kind of post hoc-script. It was only after the war that Joyce began to translate the breakdown of established norms of conduct and belief in *Finnegan's Wake*. Williams, exempted in World War I because he was a physician on duty with the local Draft Board, waited almost twenty years to record his response to America's brief participation, perhaps stimulated by his apprehension of a second cataclysm.

.   .   .   .

Although Williams is often thought to be the particular master of the short poem, the section "Longer Poems 1910–1938" in the *CCP* establishes that his interest in the long poem is not new. But there are "long" poems of three or four pages and "long" poems of book length. Williams in *Paterson* Books I and II has only recently ventured into the book-length class. In the longer poems of the *CCP* we do not discover an essentially different Williams (except in the early "The Wanderer") from the poet of the shorter ones. Indeed, many poems quite as long as the "longer" poems are not included in this section. Among those which are, "An Elegy for D. H. Lawrence," "The Flower," "March," "Paterson: Episode 17" and "The Wanderer" seem to me the most interesting. I shall deal with the last two when considering *Paterson*.

As elegiac poetry, "An Elegy for D. H. Lawrence" is

among the best produced by an American poet in our time. In its rich natural detail, its humility and compassion it is reminiscent of Whitman's "When Lilacs Last in the Dooryard Bloomed." The stately tread of the free-verse line (predominantly three-stressed and tending toward spondaic feet), sometimes lengthened here to suit the weight of the tragic material, demonstrates the plasticity of this mode in Williams' hands. The opening lines set the mood:

> Green points on the shrub
> and poor Lawrence dead.

Placing Lawrence's death against the background of spring heightens the irony of his futile attempt "to create summer from spring's decay." Seeing Lawrence's life as a "fury of labor/against waste and life's coldness" Williams discerns the bitter motivation which made him one of the

> . . . Men driven not to love
> but to the ends of the earth.

The frustration of Lawrence's search is emphasized by the scorching décor of arid Mexican plateaus exposed to the violence of "the satiric sun." Williams perceives that it was the very intensity of Lawrence's desire for love which poisoned him, for

> Febrile spring moves not to heat
> but always more slowly

and the serpent, symbol around which clustered Lawrence's quest, is seen as an elusive, narcissistic principle:

> . . . the snake
> with agate eyes leaned to the water . . .

But there is tenderness and understanding in the final judgment of Lawrence's tragic deprivation:

> Sorrow to the young
> that Lawrence has passed
> unwanted from England.
> And in the gardens forsythia
> and in the woods
> now the crinkled spicebush
> in flower.

"The Crimson Cyclamen" in memory of the poet's friend, the noted American painter Charles Demuth, will inevitably be compared to the Lawrence elegy. While the central metaphor of the growth and fruition of the crimson cyclamen as the growth and fruition of the artist is well-sustained, the tone of personal grief is, curiously enough, less evident than in the poem on Lawrence. The great elegies of the English tradition ("Lycidas," "In Memoriam") are poignant as much for the grief of the bereaved poet as for the loss of the person mourned.

"The Flower" is another long poem built around a fairly elaborate conceit. The flower is a nexus of value to which each petal makes a special contribution. One petal is the city which the poet cannot possess and in which he has "not the least part," although "For years . . . tormented by that miracle"; another petal goes back to the small barren community where the poet was born; another reaches to San Diego where strikers (?) are "kicking up the dust."

> Another petal reaches
>
> into the past, to Porto Rico
> when my mother was a child bathing in a small

> river and splashing water up on
> the yucca leaves to see them roll back pearls.

But although all these are part of *this* flower (the flower represents strands of personality valued by the poet) nevertheless

> A flower at its heart (the stamens, pistil,
> etc.) is a naked woman, about 38, just
>
> out of bed, worth looking at both for
> her body and her mind and what she has seen
>
> and done . . .

It is such a woman who clarifies for the poet his powerlessness to compete with the masters of the city. Accepting this view of his ineffectuality, he can only resort to wish:

> I plan one thing—that I could press
> buttons to do the curing of or caring for
>
> the sick that I do laboriously now by hand
> for cash, to have the time
>
> when I am fresh, in the morning, when
> my mind is clear and burning—to write

Apart from the biographical interest in the notion of a physician pressing buttons to cure the sick, the propriety of the image is striking, growing as it has out of the poet's speculations on the city: ". . . the blaze of power in which I have not the least part." Indeed, the last lines of this poem provide a useful index to Williams' diction in the middle '30's. There is the careful balance of a simple, colloquial vocabulary with a somewhat formal or "traditional" syntax. For example, there is the almost gerundive use of "the curing of or caring for" along with its subordination to the firm structural support of the formal subjunctive noun clause "that I could press" etc. The clause itself gains emphasis because it follows the caesura after "thing" while the latter word gains impact because it is preceded by the accented "one" which, together with the spondaic tendency of the whole first line, intensifies the urgency of the wish.

The skillful manipulation of the caesura is a lesson in the accommodation of emphasis to meaning. Williams often represents a long caesura by a dash to do the heavy work of the conventional colon. I suspect he prefers the dash because it does not retard the flow of the line as noticeably as the colon. In the lines above, the caesura after "burning" has the same weight as the one after "thing." Both isolate the subjunctive wish clause and leave the final phrase "to write" as a separate speech unit. Thus, this final phrase becomes almost expletive in its function.

The passage beginning "A flower, at its heart . . ." demonstrates the resourcefulness of Dr. Williams' line: the mixed iambic and spondaic feet of the hexameter (with the last syllable missing) makes for a captivating undulance:

her body and her mind and what she has seen

Comparing this line with the spondaic, monosyllabic cast of "I plan one thing . . ." illuminates the range of possibilities for the synthesis of emotional content and linear structure in Williams' firm metric. While this way of dissecting the poem may seem tedious to the reader, I must plead for it as necessary to the study of the anatomy of poetry. Once the body has been dissected, the reader is more likely to put the poem together as a working whole.

The "Longer Poems" of the *CCP* as well as *Paterson* (which I will discuss later) show Williams to be entirely capable of the effective long poem, given the motive and given the time. Williams' working habits may to some extent have determined the predominance of short poems in his work. Because of his crowded hours as a practicing pediatrician with a busy working-class practice, Williams' has often found it necessary to fit in time for writing between one patient and the next. He has a specially rigged-up typewriter arrangement in his office for this purpose. In the U.B. Collection I found many drafts and fragments of poems written on prescription blanks. Williams has rarely had extended periods free for writing with the exception of short summer vacations and some trips abroad, the last one being in 1927 when he took his sons to school in Switzerland.

It is useful to notice the difference between Williams' longer poems and those of his contemporaries. In the first place, Williams' long poems are not primarily narrative; indeed, there is little narrative content at all. This is interesting for in our time there have been few long poems which are not largely narrative in cast. For example, I wonder whether it is commonly noticed just how much "story" there is in *The Waste Land*. In Yeats too we often find a cunning infusion of a heavy narrative line in poems which, like "The Tower," for example, at first glance seem preeminently lyrical. In Williams' long poems the narrative element is almost always subordinate. Thus, Williams' longer poems cannot claim the suspense values, the psychological hold over the reader's curiosity which even a fragmentary knowledge of "characters" (Lil in *The Wasteland* is a good example) can exert.

Another common ingredient of the longer poem which is absent in Williams' is the didactic element. Williams' poems are often speculative in temper but whatever indoctrination they may accomplish is achieved only incidentally. The absence of two familiar elements in the long poem, story and moral discourse, as well as the fact that Williams' lyricism is a stark one, unwilling to make concessions in the way of predictable "beauty" may explain why his longer poems are seldom discussed. Sometimes, however, other elements, notably the satiric impulse, can become involved with the primary lyric intention. When this occurs, narrative is likely to appear. This will be seen in *Paterson*.

.   .   .   .

The Broken Span, a slim pamphlet of poems, appeared in 1941. Inaccuracies are inevitable in evaluating them, for while some are dated as far back as 1915 and 1927, others are undated and in no poem is there any indication when the final version was made. Judging from internal evidence, I should say all the poems had been recently revised even when, as in "The Suckers," dated 1927, the content would appear to be topical—a critique of American justice motivated by the then raging Sacco-Vanzetti case.

THE POEMS

"A Love Song" with the subtitle "First Version: 1915" suggests by its imagistic manner that the present version may be taken as a satire on an earlier attitude. It is a successful love lyric, the subjective sexual connotations which are infused into landscape working with particular effectiveness. Contradictory terms are used to express two sides of a familiar equation (love), thus destroying the predictable order of experience and, at the same time, evoking the chaotic state of the lovers: "I am alone/The weight of love/Has buoyed me up/Till my head knocks against the sky." The paradox of *weight* as *buoyant* prepares us to accept the fairy-tale fancy of the lover's head touching the sky. Love has upset categories.

In "A Marriage Ritual" (1928) there is a similar interaction of mood with landscape. The internal rime suggests recent re-working. The poet is wedded to a city which does not recognize him and the poem as a whole is interesting chiefly as a preliminary exercise of the later *Paterson* theme. Related to "A Marriage Ritual" is a sequence of fifteen brief sketches titled "For the Poem Paterson." Many of these have been utilized in the final version and their proper consideration belongs with the discussion of *Paterson*.

Among the most successful poems of this slender collection are "The Last Words of My English Grandmother" and "A Portrait of the Times," both examples of a critical realism articulated with a clinical detachment. In "The Last Words" the meticulous objectivity of the portrait creates an old woman as "real" as a Rembrandt, but without the chiarascuro. Williams' uncanny rendering of the querulous speech of the old, of their resistant cupidity

99

toward death, elevates this plain talk into a subtle commentary on a universal predicament:

> Let me take you to the hospital, I said
> and after you are well
> you can do as you please.
> She smiled, Yes
> you do what you please first
> then I can do what I please—

. . . .

When in 1944, a new volume of Williams' poems, *The Wedge,* appeared, an "Author's Introduction" lent the transaction a characteristic flavor:

The war is the first and only thing in the world today. The arts generally are not, nor is this writing a diversion from that for relief, a turning away. It is the war or part of it, merely a different sector of the field . . . The making of poetry is no more an evidence of frustration than is the work of Henry Kaiser or Timoshenko. It's the war, the driving forward of desire to a complex end . . . The arts have a common relation to society . . .

With characteristic defiance, Williams ends by saying that if the poet's interest in taking words as he "finds them interrelated about him" and composing them into "an intense expression of his perception and ardors that they constitute a revelation in the speech he uses," represents "preart" then it is along those lines he seeks development. This passage emphasizes Williams' respect for *live* tradition (here usage in speech) as well as his wish to create a "revelation" within its boundaries. The "traditional" content in Williams' language remarked by Yvor Winters flows from this motive.

100

THE POEMS

In *The Wedge* individual poems reiterate various aspects of this aesthetic. The opening "A Sort of a Song," utilizing a refrain from "Paterson: Episode 17" ("No ideas but in things") stresses the necessity of the poet to invent—to make "things." In "Catastrophic Birth" the prerequisites for such making, whether in art or in nature, are implied by the related events of the erupting volcano and the childering "she-Wop":

> Each age brings new calls upon violence
> for new rewards, variants of the old.

An awesome illumination of this bare syllogism is achieved by the images of the drunkard, the only survivor of the eruption, and the old woman who "at a touch . . . falls into a heap of ashes." The drunkard, saved by violence because he was previously "underground," seems to represent the artist as maker, while the old woman, caught in her ritual hair-combing, and falling apart at a touch, represents the body of art which, tried and habitual, moulders because it lacks the vitality necessary for "catastrophic birth."

That I have not stretched the implications of this severe exposure of the violence of creativity is confirmed by "To All Gentleness," a fine poem, which resolves what Williams feels to be the false opposition of the poetic and the antipoetic, a concocted paradox, from which, as I have indicated, the understanding of his own work has suffered. Seeming antinomies are found to be complementary: thus we have the lion lying down with the lamb, the wrecked airman's wound succored by the very sea which would engulf him, and

101

> Out of fear lest the flower be broken
> the rose puts out its thorns. That
> is the natural way.

The flower, as symbol, embraces the others: "The flower is our sign." The idea of the "anti-poetic" then is merely a naïve dissociation of what is organic to the "poetic": Sand and rubble premise the flower, "without which, no flower."

A whimsical version of this approach is developed in the gay "The Poem" in which the poet advises that a song be made of "particulars." That Williams heeds his own advice is perceptible: we find the evidence in the haunting refrain of "The Hounded Lovers" ("Where shall we go?/ Where shall we go/who are in love?"); in the jovial measures of "The Dance," about Breughel's great painting, "The Kermess," where the skillfully disposed internal rimes contribute to the ingenious run-on pattern; in the muted ballad structure of "The Gentle Negress" ("Wandering among the chimneys/my love and I would meet/I with a pale skin/she as brown as peat"); in the affectionate and robust concreteness of "To Ford Madox Ford in Heaven," and in the small brilliant distinctness of "The Yellow Chimney."

But occasional failures in *The Wedge* caused by an over-reliance on the formula of earlier successes in particularity, coupled with a restlessness exhibited in Williams' exploration of end-rhyme, half-rhyme, internal-rhyme, refrain, echo, ballad structure, etc., hint at a stock-taking during the war years. It must be remembered that the plays preliminary to and included in *Trial Horse No. 1* were written during this time, and *Paterson* was being carefully plotted. But that Williams did wish to test other modes of poetic communication is further indicated in the epigrammatic wit of "A Plea for Mercy" and of "In Sisterly Fashion." Both are modifications of traditional forms. The first employs the quatrain mold of the classical epigram but omits the rhyme; the second suggests a ballad scaffolding accommodated to epigrammatic content.

The most adventurous poem in *The Wedge* is "The Monstrous Marriage" which relates a curious dreamlike allegory in an easy colloquial diction. The "story" is of a strange mating: a woman tends a wounded pigeon which infects her with its own pain, while it turns to a hawk in her hands.

> After that
> she adopted a hawk's life as her own.
> For it looked up and said, You are
> my wife for this . . .

Later, the bird complains that his head is "mostly . . . clouded except for hunting . . ." and when it becomes "clear . . . by your love." The woman will not concede this defect in him, but the hawk is desolate, knowing his nature:

> Nestling upon her as was his wont he
> hid his talons from her soft flesh
> fluttering his wings against her sides

But there is the world's view of such a monstrous marriage and the hawk must be off when footsteps are heard:

> After that she had a leather belt made
> upon which he perched to enjoy her.

103

The archaic dignity of the poem is entirely dependent on the sustained fable. There is no subjective interpretation whatsoever. That this interesting study is an off-shoot of Williams' ever deepening inquiries into the nature of love, so strikingly revealed in his recent plays, is clear.

On the whole, *The Wedge*, apart from its visible explorations of the possibilities of rhyme, seems a consolidation of Williams' achievements rather than an expansion of them. His preoccupations are the familiar ones: art, value, the value of art, the art of value,

> —through metaphor to reconcile
> The people and the stones.

. . . .

The Clouds, published in 1948, four years after *The Wedge*, is a collection of sixty poems, many of them very short and, I suspect, by-products of Williams' work on *Paterson*. Like *The Wedge*, *The Clouds* does not reveal any new dimension of Williams' sensibility and confirms rather than reshapes his achievement. But where *The Wedge* was impressive largely for its technical probings, *The Clouds* in its best poems is memorable for a deepened tone of speculation, of inquiry into the nature of love, death and immortality. As I shall point out when discussing *Paterson*, Books I and II, where Williams considers these issues within the context of a cultural setting, he has found an order-making, although not a novel answer to his quest. But here in the more personal poetry, unsupported by the objective narrative frame of *Paterson*, the issues are closer to the surface. Many poems are suffused by an awareness of the proximity of death, as is the later poetry of Yeats and Eliot. But where Yeats is anguished and violent, Williams, without the support of dogma, manages an effect of calm and integration similar to Eliot's. But Williams' resignation differs in this: it is got without any mystical test. He is concerned with the pitch of experience in the world as he lives in it. The certainty of a future life, if one had it, would offer no solution for him to this world's dilemmas.

"Russia" is a loosely organized poem with some brilliant passages. It exhibits a fault in Williams which is rare, but when present, distracting. It was shown most flagrantly in the early improvisations of *Kora in Hell*. There, as we saw, it took the form of posing about the role of the artist, a self-conscious nose-thumbing at those who refused to follow Puck. Here it is the same fault although now the mood is not defiant, but rather one of a false humility unbecoming to Williams' genuine achievements.

The poet asks Russia to look through his eyes in order to understand his dream of her. He says:

> . . . I am
> a poet, a stupid, uninfluential poet, excluded
> from anthologies, with no skill
> in polemics—my friends tell me I lack
> the intellect . . .

In the end, Williams mutes the intended irony by the condition on which he dedicates his dreams to Russia "now when I am about to die." Poets have, of course, before underestimated both their accomplishments and the condition of their health. But in Williams this seems an affectation for it is out of line with the disciplined absence of self-pity in the larger part of his work. Reference

105

to his impending death is false, too, on the poem's own terms: the superiority of a dream that was Russia to the reality that Russia is, is the real theme of the poem:

> O Russia, Russia! must we begin to call
> you the idiot of the world? When
> you were a dream the world lived in you
> inviolate—

The poet invites the real Russia into his dream, but, at the same time, he calls himself "undistinguished,/of no moment." He wishes both to be host and also to serve as doormat: "I am the background/upon which you will build your empire." The two wishes are contradictory; the first cancels the second, and vice versa. The result is sentiment. The cause of the poem's confusion is a confusion in thinking, manifested, at the poetic level, as a confusion in feeling. This happens not because Williams has not the intellect, but because on the subject of an old dream he finds hard to relinquish he has not been careful to use it. The tone of the poem is nostalgic, reproachful, as if addressed to a treacherous mistress; it is the tone of a man who has been, in spite of himself, fooled by his dream.

"The Visit" is a moving rationale of Williams' present aesthetic and ethical position. The theme develops through an implied metaphor of which the sea is the inclusive background. The friend to whom the poem is addressed (the tone is informally discursive) has apparently held up a mode of poetry which the poet rejects:

> Let us resume. The
> naive may be like a sunny day but
> deceptive

and not to be despised
because it is so amusing to see
the zigzag and slender gulls
dip into the featureless surface.
It is fish they are after,
fish—and get them.
    Still I
acknowledge the sea is there and
I admire its profundity only
what does that amount to?
Love also may be deep, deep
as thought, deeper than thought
and as sequential—

"The featureless surface" brilliantly describes a deliberate archaic flatness which characterizes some of Williams' poetry, particularly that of his Objectivist period. But just as the purposiveness of the gulls—they do get the fish they are after—is what gives the lie to their seemingly playful behavior, so the poet may be dredging up a catch not transparently visible on the "featureless surface" of the poem.

Running parallel to the profundity of the sea (imagination) is the profundity of love, "deep as thought, deeper than thought and as sequential." The pure entelechy, the deep sequentiality of love, are the values which Williams would oppose as complementary to "thought/ full of detail . . . as/ the courts are full of law and the sea weeds and/ as murmurous . . ." Suddenly, in a violent outburst of pride which temporarily abandons the sea imagery of the poem the poet exclaims:

Say I am less an artist
than a spadeworker but one

who has no aversion to taking
his spade to the head
of any who would derogate
his performance in the craft.

The poem ends with a formal thanks tendered to the friend "for the view" but underneath there is a hard and just resistance to any attempt, however well-meaning, which seeks to inject into the artist's horizon what is not *sui generis* to his intention.

Like the recent plays, like *Paterson*, "A History of Love," as its title suggests, is about the ages of love. The first lines, apparently addressed to a child, argue that flowers grow with the help of the coarsest waste. The order to the child when a horse passes "Out with you then, dustpan and broom" to "gather turds for your grandmother's garden," by its organic imagery is meant to implement the poem's plea: to fertilize love by *any* agency. In the next section, the poet stresses the loveliness and "its counter-hell" which can be projected into the world of art (here the pages of a book being read) and enlarged by imagination into a vision "to confound the mind." While the poet speaks to some loved person, in effect he chastises his own timidity toward letting the image of love take full possession. Section III implies by its syntax a lapse of time during which love has flourished but has already begun to die. It enjoins:

With the mind and with the hand
by moral turn and prestidigitation
fan the smouldering flame of love
which in the dull coals is all but gone.

THE POEMS

The hope is to rouse

> the banished smile that used to spring
> at once at meeting!

Any expedient which will reawaken love is valid as the anti-poetic injunction of the first stanza hinted. Now, the same affirmation is invoked—although liberated from its original imagery—in the moving couplet which ends the poem:

> For flowers are not, as we are not
> of that stuff, whence we both are got.

Still, one feels a renunciatory undertone beneath the firm structure of the lines.

"The Clouds" surveys such phenomena of mortality to ask, in effect, what is the teleology of decay. "Where are the good minds of past days, the unshorn?" Williams asks, naming Villon, Erasmus, Shakespeare, Aristotle, Aristophanes, and Socrates, "Plato's better self."

> They all, like Aristophanes, knew the clouds and
> said next to nothing of the soul's flight
> but kept their heads and died—

They live in "their relics, ourselves." The poet contrasts these "truth-tellers" with those who now seek to deny mortality through various expedients—for example, spiritualism:

> as if the certainty of a future life
> were any solution to our dilemma . . .

In Section III, "Scherzo," the delightful presence of a priest in Amalfi "jiggling upon his buttocks to the litany" while "riding the clouds of his belief," is invoked. The warmth of this portrayal establishes Williams' tolerance for any "cloud" of belief which the individual can joyously mount.

But for himself Williams chooses a sterner doctrine, perhaps best described as a restatement of the Aristotelian emphasis on potentiality or individuation in the human psyche:

> Thus each
> is valued by what he carries and that is his soul—
> diminishing the bins by that much
> unless replenished.

The honorable ancestry of Williams' understanding of the soul is illuminated by this definition from *De Anima*:

We have stated generally what soul is; it is the substance, so far as this is expressible in a definition, i.e., the essence, of a body of a certain kind, just as, if some tool—e.g., an axe—were a natural body, its axeness would be its substance and this would be its soul, and if this were taken away it would no longer be an axe except in an equivocal sense.

And, if the pagan nexus of Williams' thinking here needs further explication, it is through the title itself, suggesting as it does Aristophanes' *The Clouds,* the point of whose satire is to ridicule Plato's philosophy (in the person of Socrates) and especially his Ideal Forms. The counter-theme "But if they live? What then?" again crops up at the end to be finally put down: the confusion of the world man knows (as opposed to the "no-knowledge of their nameless destiny") must still be dealt with, the "straining" mind, and the flesh itself "in which the poet foretells his own death." The clouds (now become a symbol for the shifting, phantasmagoric character of experience) are still there, perpetually to perplex and challenge.

THE POEMS

If these comments have stressed the matrix of this collection as speculative in temper, I should add that among peripheral graces are many poems with that matter-of-fact understatement which marks Williams' special mode of wit. Among these is "The Horse" which slyly constructs an analogy between the horse who has eyes like a woman and "is generally conscious of the world" yet "pulls when he must and pulls well" and the equal vanities and resiliencies of the female sex. There is too that small masterpiece of narrative humor, "For a Low Voice," detailing the confusion of the city fathers when, in digging down into the graves of the old Dutch cemetery to make a city park, they could not even find a single thigh-bone, a situation which created a

> shall we say? dilemma. So that,
> to make a gesture, for old time's sake,
> heh, heh! of filling
> the one vault retained as communal repository
>
> huh, huh! and monument, they
> had to throw in SOMETHING! presumed
> to be bones but observed by those nearest,
> heh, heh, heh! more to resemble
>
> rotten tree roots than *ossa!*
>   . . .

The moral of this predicament, as the first stanza points out, is that "If you ignore the possibilities of art . . . you are likely to become involved in extreme . . . difficulties." Williams' didacticism, usually held below the surface of his poems by the austerity of his technique, is as operative upon the trivia of daily experience as it is upon the "cosmic" issues. *The Clouds* emphasizes the persistence in Williams of that ethicalizing strain which was fostered well into his twenties by his Unitarian upbringing.

. . . .

A poem not included in *The Clouds,* but dating contemporaneously with many which are, is "The Pink Church," which shares with the longer poems I have just discussed their profoundly religious mood of self-examination. Dream as more "real" than reality ("Russia"), love more profound than thought ("The Visit"), these are themes, as we shall see in *Paterson* and *A Dream of Love* which recur with greater frequency in Williams' recent work. In "The Pink Church," which at first appears uncharacteristic of Williams, these themes are resolved into a swelling hymn of affirmation. Conceived as a chorale, its eminent singability is revealed in the fine setting which has been made for it by Celia Thaew. The melodic line without piano accompaniment may be found in the Williams' Issue of the *Briarcliff Quarterly,* October 1946.

The poem begins with a description of the singer's first experience of beauty (imagination) which came to him through religious channels:

> —and tho' I remember little
>   as names go,
> the thrust of that first light
>   was to me
>   as through a heart of jade
> as Chinese as you please
> but not by that—remote.

The illumination was memorable for its immediacy rather than for any ritual through which it was canalized:

now the Pink Church (vision of revelation) "trembles/to the light (of dawn) again," and demands expression in song. The "rigors" of this compelling call to absolution are implicit in the message it would pit against a conception of man as sinful: "Man is not sinful . . . unless he sin!" All the "aberrant"—drunks, prostitutes, Surrealists, and "Proust's memory (in a cork diving suit)"—are asked to bear witness to this. For are not

> —Poe, Whitman, Baudelaire
> the saints of this calendar.

It is in man that we must place our faith. "Who else?" asks the poet, urging the expansion of the "delights" of man's nature into all the aspects of joyous creativity. Even the philosophers who, at the least, have the perspicacity to wonder "at the nature/of the stuff/poured into/the urinals/of custom . . ." are urged to "teach well!" for above their teaching stands the Pink Church

> the nipples of
> a woman who never
> bore a
> child . . .

The Pink Church, then, is immaculate, non-utilitarian beauty and good. How can we again possess this good, we who, unlike the fool, the deranged, the suicide, the slaughtered and the lonely, have had no glimpse of the delight vouchsafed to them in

> the holy church of
> their minds, singing madly
> in tune, its stones
> sibilant and roaring—

113

This authenticity of vision, this closer accessibility to revelation which Williams, like Yeats, tends to assign to the "unfit," to the Crazy Janes of our times, is a growingly stubborn note in his later work, as it was in that of the Irish poet. A distinction must, of course, be drawn between Williams' and Yeats' endorsements of these types. Yeats values the Crazy Janes and the Lunatic Toms for a supposed superior vitality at the source of their emphasis on "experience." Williams values them for a supposed superior perception of a spiritually conceived joyousness or affirmation. Thus do the dynamics of art destroy our classifications. The "materialist" Williams in his old age yearns toward a mystical, prophetic position while Yeats, the willful "obscurantist," tends toward a realism which embraces the generative good of *all* vitality.

We are then reminded of the martyrdom of Michael Servitus and thus of all those who have suffered for idea. We are urged to be perfect "even as your/Father in Heaven/is perfect" or as "perfect as the pink and/rounded breasts of a virgin." The differences between the symbols chosen for perfection imply a greater flexibility in the scheme of value than we had first sensed. The crucial need is constancy to a vision of perfection whether in the ecclesiastical terms of a perfect Father in Heaven, or in the secular terms of perfect beauty represented by the rounded breast of a virgin. The poet would shout a message of

> Joy! Joy!
> —out of Elysium!

THE POEMS

The final stanza, with its powerful allusion to "Milton the unrhymer" a heretic who stuck to his vision of good, like Samson:

> singing among
> the rest . . .
>
> like a Communist.

winds up the crashing orchestration into a rich resolution where past and present merge into a triumphant whole. It is no accident that stanza one opens with the pink light of a dawn in Galilee and the last ends with Milton, singing. The absolution hinted at early in the poem has now been fortified and raised into a triumphant vindication of the rightness of man's fidelity to his own vision of integrity (the mention of *Samson Agonistes* supports this reading), however rebellious that dedication may superficially appear.

* * * *

Books I and II of *Paterson,* the first installments of the modern epic poem which Williams projected for several decades, have evoked considerable critical acclaim since their recent publication. It is already evident that in conception and execution *Paterson* is Williams' most ambitious poetic undertaking. In my discussion of Books I and II, I shall be collating the final published version with earlier published fragments, as well as with MS notes in the U.B. Collection, and with the interestingly emended galley proofs of the final version. In this way, although the reader will perforce be limited to the early published fragments, and the final poem, we may arrive at a richer reading of *Paterson*. Wherever useful, I shall indicate the precise source to which I refer.

The industrial town of Paterson is situated on the Passaic River in northeast New Jersey. While built chiefly on a plain surrounded on the north and west by high hills, a part of the town lies on the high point where the river descends over the Passaic Falls. With a population of about 140,000 partly composed of many first- and second-generation Central European stocks, Paterson is a distinctly working-class, industrial community. It is often called "The Lyons of America" because it is the principle silk manufacturing center of the Western hemisphere.

But the Paterson of the poem transcends the "real" Paterson. The city is seen as an image of and for man. An Author's Note to Book I outlines the projected work as follows: "Part One introduces the elemental character of the place. The Second Part will comprise the modern replicas. Three will seek a language to make them vocal, and Four, the river below the falls, will be reminiscent of episodes—all that one man may achieve in a lifetime." The river thus becomes the stream of history. Through the Paterson symbol Williams seeks to elevate the local or "place" to the status of the universal. Of the four books, I, "The Delineaments of the Giants," is an investigation of the sources of the "place."

In an attempt to orient the reader to the various languages of the poem, Williams has appended a passage from John Addington Symonds' *Studies of the Greek Poets* which elucidates the practise of Hipponax who tried

. . . to bring the meter still more within the sphere of prose or common speech . . . by their acceptance of this halting meter, the Greeks displayed their aesthetic sense of propriety, recognizing the harmony which subsists between crabbed verses and distorted subjects with which they dealt—the vices and perversions of humanity . . .

While Mr. Yvor Winters would no doubt term Hipponax' practice "the fallacy of imitative form," there is little question but that some good verse has been written on this principle. The real point at issue in Williams' quotation of authority, a sanction he rarely invokes, is not so much that he wishes to bring "the meter still more within the sphere of prose or common speech" as that he is eager to promote his own speech, a speech which, as a reading of *Paterson* will show, is neither prose nor common speech, but sometimes assimilates elements from both.

The italicized paragraph preceding the Preface of *Paterson*, Book I states the intention of the poem. A heraldic trumpet note spreads out into a firm, rich music:

a local pride; spring, summer, fall and the sea; a confession, a basket; a column, a reply to Greek and Latin with the bare hands; a gathering up; a celebration;
in distinctive terms; by multiplication a reduction to one; daring; a fall; the clouds resolved into a sandy sluice; an enforced pause;
hard put to it; an identification and a plan for action to supplant a plan for action; a taking up of slack; a dispersal and a metamorphosis.

The Preface, containing some of the finest lines in the poem, stands in place of the conventional invocation to the muse in classical epic. It describes the poet's attitude toward his materials while, at the same time, it leads the

117

reader directly into the milieu of *Paterson*. It restates the grounding of Williams' earlier work in a hard, clipped line. The whole is, in effect, the metaphysic of his "local pride."

> To make a start,
> out of particulars
> and make them general, rolling
> up the sum, by defective means—
> Sniffing the trees,
> just another dog
> among a lot of dogs. What
> else is there? And to do?
> The rest have run out—
> after the rabbits.
> Only the lame stands—on
> three legs. Scratch front and back.
> Deceive and eat. Dig
> a musty bone
>
> For the beginning is assuredly
> the end—since we know nothing, pure
> and simple, beyond
> our own complexities.

The last four lines will inevitably recall the leitmotif of Eliot's *Four Quartets*, "In my beginning is my end." But the clause "since we know nothing" reverses the philosophical implications of the assertion that "the beginning is assuredly the end" and reduces it to an ironical tautology. We do know something but only those things which can be known through our own complexities. This does not mean, however, that we know our own complexities. The sense of "beyond" is outside of, rather than beside.

In the next lines the city, the man—"an identity"—are seen as "an/interpenetration, both ways . . . the drunk, the sober; the illustrious/the gross; one. In ignorance a certain knowledge and knowledge, undispersed, its own undoing." The habit of mind which loses sight of the flux in experience is scorned, for:

> . . . never in this
> world will a man live well in his body
> save dying—and not know himself
> dying; that is
> the design. Renews himself
> thereby, in addition and subtraction,
> walking up and down.

The poet scorns alike the writing of stale poems and the rigid dogmatism of "Minds like beds always made up/ (more stoney than a shore)." The word "shore" catapults us right into the clatter and thrust of the Falls; we go "from mathematics to particulars—," to dew, shells, animalcules,

> . . . and so to man,
> to Paterson.

Thus we arrive at the first of the three parts of *The Delineaments of the Giants* whose total structure is analogous to the movement of the river "that flows and encircles."

In the opening lines Paterson is presented as a giant. Later, his identity shimmers and metamorphoses into that of the poet, the citizens, and the city. Sometimes, he is the poet-citizen; elsewhere, he becomes the thoughts of the poet, "Mr. Paterson," "sitting and standing." Paterson, then, is a great fictive generator. He is both myth and the maker of myth. He is the city lying in the valley under the Passaic Falls. He is asleep, immobile, "Butterflies

119

settle on his stone ear" yet "his dreams walk about the city where he persists/incognito." Paterson is procreator and, miraculously, he is the child of his own imaginings as well.

There are the automatons animated by the giant-Paterson (in this aspect Paterson is the city, an industrial dynamo generated by the Falls) "who neither know their sources nor the sills of their/disappointments walk outside their bodies aimlessly . . ./locked and forgot in their desires—unroused." As if fearful that this analysis will have blurred his focus the poet admonishes himself: "Say it, no ideas but in things—." This will be recognized as an incorporation from the "Paterson" of the *CCP,* with the significant but plot-revealing omission of three imperfect lines: "These are the ideas, savage and tender/ somewhat of the music, etcetera/of Paterson, that great philosopher." Now the leitmotif of "no ideas but in things" branches into an itemization of things: trees, houses, spires, and thence to the river in its primitive energy pouring in above the city. Parenthetically, the poet wonders "What common language to unravel?/from that rafter of a rock's lip." This question is left unanswered and we are introduced to "the archaic persons of the drama" who, in a deleted passage in the galleys, are described as:

> A man like a city and a woman like a flower
> who are in love. Two women. Three women.
> Innumerable women, each like a flower.

There follows an excerpt from a letter written to the poet-Paterson by a woman who pathetically asks him to return her poems without comment "if you should find that embarrassing—for it was the human situation and not the literary one that motivated my phone calls and visit. Besides, I know myself to be more the woman than the poet. . . ." Keeping the analogy of the circular, eddying movement of the poem before one, it becomes clear that the prose letter represents one of the "women, like a flower, who are in love." There will be others.

The next lines support this reading. Soon another woman appears stretched "against him" (Paterson). It is the low mountain, facing him, his "arm supporting her . . . asleep." In a brief prose passage rather like an old-fashioned guide book or a provincial paper's "Historical" column occurs the account of a local shoemaker who in 1857 began collecting mussels in which he discovered pearls, an event which initiated a great pearl hunt. This tale, the first of a series of fine vignettes, initiates the exploration of Paterson's past, "all one." This passage also explains the earlier reference to the mountain with "pearls at her ankles."

It is necessary to remember that throughout *Paterson* the prose meaning and the poetic meaning are intended to supplement one another. The prose provides an order of data which the poetry explores for meaning, idea and tone. But the two levels of discourse are not distinct (except typographically) for there is a continual structural and thematic interlacing.

The poem turns from the anecdotal pearl hunt of 1857 to the contemporary Mr. Paterson, now presumably the poet *of* Paterson. But the harsh leitmotif interrupts:

> Say it! No ideas but in things. Mr.
> Paterson has gone away

> to rest and write. Inside the bus one sees
> his thoughts sitting and standing . . .

In an oddly subjective passage the multiple personality of Paterson is developed under his *human* aspect. The shifting syntax of the lines, the fluidity of the pronouns which exchange case and number make for a symbiosis of all the facets of Paterson:

> Who are these people (how complex
> the mathematic) among whom I see myself
> in the regularly ordered plateglass of
> his thoughts, glimmering before shoes and bicycles?
>   They walk incommunicado, the
> equation is beyond solution, yet
> its sense is clear—that they may live
> his thought is listed in the Telephone
> Directory—

An amusing return to the past is contrived, for our ancestors "craved the miraculous," not, it is implied, "the regularly ordered plateglass" thoughts of the modern hero. A prose bulletin tells of the ethnic stocks represented in the city of Paterson from the past century to the present, in another attempt to discover its sources. When we have read Books I and II of *Paterson* we are left with a richer sociology of Paterson than a series of monographs could provide. For it is precisely the selection and the contiguity of concrete detail which discloses the American grain of Paterson. It is this fresh discrimination of *relationships* which makes the poem sociologically and historically valid, while, at the same time, as an aesthetic whole it surpasses what could be constructed independently on either of those grounds.

Suddenly we are back in the present with "Marriage come to have a shuddering implication." A few girls from "families that have decayed and taken to the hills" go to the Coast without gain:

> The language is missing them
> they die also
> incommunicado
>
> The language, the language
> fails them

The "torrent in their minds . . . is foreign to them" for "the language is divorced from their minds,/the language . . . the language!" The changes Williams rings with his echo device are varied, ranging from irony to a delicate nostalgia. We understand why the people are divorced from a language when we see the background of violence, degradation and incest which, "under the calm trees," gave birth to the declassed descendants of Indians, Negroes, Hessian deserters and English prostitutes known as Jackson's Whites.[11]

Because the imagination demands refreshment from the sordid assault of the present, we are presented with the

[11] I have mentioned the Jackson Whites in my discussion of "To Elsie." Jackson was a man "under contract with the British government to provide women for the soldiers in America" during the Revolutionary War. In addition to the strains I noted, Williams writes that "Cromwell, in the middle of the Seventeenth Century, shipped some thousand of Irish women and children to the Barbados to be sold as slaves. Forced by their owners to mate with the others these unfortunates were succeeded by a generation of Irish-speaking negroes and mulattoes. And it is commonly asserted to this day that the natives of Barbados speak with an Irish brogue." The region in New Jersey of which Williams speaks is New Barbados Neck, near Paterson.

memorable picture of a primitive and vigorous sexuality in a vital and coordinated society, whose members were, perhaps, among the remote ancestors of the depraved Jackson's Whites. It is the picture seen in the *Geographic* of the nine women of some African chief, semi-naked, astraddle a log, heads left:

> Foremost
> froze the young and latest
> erect, a proud queen, conscious of her power,
> mud-caked, her monumental hair
> slanted above the brows—violently frowning
>
> Behind her, packed tight up
> in a descending scale of freshness
> stiffened the others
> . . .

We see them all, the breasts of the first wife "sagging from hard use," and are led to consider the "rekindling" bespoken by the "up-pointed breasts of that other . . ." This is Williams at his best: the general implicit in the particular, the language pure and firm to fit the primitive vigor of the subject, the interpretation suppressed but the poem nevertheless begetting its own urgent morality. The contrast between the leveling and barren present and the fecundity of a primitive society, graded in terms of natural vitality, is established by juxtaposing the African women to the girls from "decayed families" where marriage has come to have a "shuddering implication." The tragic descent in scale and function is undeniable.

The record of this descent in Paterson's history is now documented by the prose accounts of the lives of various citizens who responded to the "pouring language" (the vitality) of the Falls. There is the bride who in 1812 disappeared into the Falls while being instructed in the beauties of the place by her husband; there is Sam Patch, the Old-time Jersey Patriot, boss of cotton spinners in one of the mills, who, with drunkard's courage, makes a brilliant jump from the Falls which establishes him as local hero. "There's no mistake in Sam Patch!" He knew the water, "filling his ears with sound, hard to interpret," called for something great and he jumped. Patch became a famous jumper all through the country, leaping from greater heights each time, until he undertook one final, thrilling leap of 125 feet from the falls of the Genesee River. But "He struck the water on his side and disappeared," for "Speech had failed him. He was confused. The word had been drained of its meaning." Sam, in deserting his local good, had failed as local god. Divorced from his roots, his impulse toward the miraculous in action becomes merely automatic, a meaningless repetition of skill: "The word . . . drained of its meaning."

Part II expands the elegiac note of Sam's special failure into a fuller mourning: "There is no direction . . . The how (the howl) only/is at my disposal (proposal) . . ." Williams is saying there is only solitary, fragmentary good (beauty) but this is inadequate because unhallowed by the communion essential to a whole humanity:

> a bud forever green,
> tight-curled, upon the pavement, perfect
> in juice and substance but divorced, divorced
> from its fellows, fallen low—

> Divorce is
> the sign of knowledge in our time,
> divorce! divorce!

The dismal echo "divorce! divorce!" re-enforces "The how (the howl)" so that irony, hopelessness, and an ineffectual rage at the hopelessness itself is begot. The equation illustrates how flexibly Williams manages this type of modified refrain. Divorce from language, divorce from marriage, reverse faces of the social coin—this may not be a hopeful reading of the times but it seems an accurate one. Still, from this chord of melancholy knowledge, the poet derives a lyric passage of considerable beauty in the scene of the "Two half-grown girls hailing hallowed Easter, . . . Their clear hair dangling—":

> one—
> a willow twig pulled from a low
> leafless bush in full bud in her hand,
> (or eels or a moon!)
> holds it, the gathered spray,
> upright in the air, the pouring air,
> strokes the soft fur—
>
> Aint they beautiful!

The artlessness of this clear writing, the chaste simplicity of the picture as in a primitive Greek frieze, the parenthetical "(or eels or a moon!)" subtly effecting a fertility association—all this hardly prepares one for the wry pathos of "Aint they beautiful!" The full, rich vowels and liquid sounds of "willow," "low," "eels," "moon," as well as the joyous repetition of "the air, the pouring air," heighten, by contrast, the pitiful impoverishment of the girls' reverent "Aint they beautiful!"

126

THE POEMS

The narrator admits he does not know how to identify the altered ground of the present. He even questions the meaningfulness of the concept of personality, his *own* personality:

> Why even speak of "I," he dreams, which
> interests me almost not at all?
>
> The theme
> is as it may prove: asleep, unrecognized—

Suddenly, he has a vision of what his task is and even perceives a method for it:

> . . . a mass of detail
> to interrelate on a new ground, difficultly;
> an assonance, a homologue
>
> triple piled
> pulling the disparate together to clarify
> and compress

A crisp summoning up of river-connected imagery now precipitates another antiphonal strand of speculation:

> The thought returns: Why have I not
> but for imagined beauty where there is none
> or none available, long since
> put myself deliberately in the way of death?

The anti-poetic answer to this rhetoric is given in the disdainful mockery of the next line:

> Stale as a whale's breath: breath!
> Breath!

The identification of death with the stale breath of a whale fuses in the poet's mind the separate deaths of Mrs. Cummins and Sam Patch and he is led to a sad confession:

127

> Only of late, late! begun to know, to
> know clearly (as through clear ice) whence
> I draw my breath or how to employ it
> clearly, if not well:

The phrase "as through clear ice" is an example of how resourcefully the symbols are worked in *Paterson*. It was Sam Patch whose body was found in the Spring "frozen in an ice-cake." Now, it is the poet who sees his own past as a rigid, congealed body without "breath."

The other themes of the poem now re-enter the consciousness of the narrator: the African first wife "her old thighs/gripping the log reverently, that, all of a piece, holds up the others," the "two sisters from whose open mouths/Easter is born . . ." He recognizes that his sources are "certainly Not the university," for there too is divorce, the "language stutters"; rather

> While
> the green bush sways: is whence
> I draw my breath . . .
>
>   . . .
>
> Which is to say, though it be poorly
> said, there is a first wife
> and a first beauty, complex, ovate—
> and woody sepals standing back under
> the stress to hold it there, innate
>
> a flower within a flower whose history
> (within the mind) crouching
> among the ferny rocks, laughs at the names
> by which they think to trap it. Escapes!

This grows into a powerful attack on "learning" in which the persistent change and metamorphosis of natural forms is used as counterfoil to "the whole din of fracturing thought." All is rejected. But the poet admits "the partic-ular/no less vague." A less vague "reality" is then con-sidered, a hope for communion through sex, recognizing there is "no language . . . to seize the moment."

Now, concealed monologue (a form which we saw Williams was partial to in his early work) is woven into the poem's predominantly lyric texture in such a way that it takes on a lyric quality. The melodic line is am-plified by the setting, a river-bank, where the lover makes his imagined declaration:

> I wish to be with you abed, we two
> as if the bed were the bed of a stream

But instead the lovers sit and talk and the

> silence speaks of the giants
> who have died in the past and have
> returned to those scenes unsatisfied
> and who is not unsatisfied . . .

This complicated relationship (the woman has consented to others "too swiftly") is united with the major thematic strands of *Paterson*: the no-language motif (here the stream has "no language"), the our-sources-not-known-to-us motif (here the "giants" live in the woman's acknowl-edged desire), the "separate worlds" motif (here a natural competitiveness "the birds against the fish," "the brambles in the blossom"). The basic male, female symbols of *Paterson* (stream, falls, rocks) function as a huge loom-ing backdrop of mood and emotion which not only unify the action but are themselves intertwined as agents in the pattern of events. Finally, the poet, confused by the multiplicity of possible explanations, theories *about* life ("A delirium of solutions"), is forced into "back streets, to begin again." He is forced to a revision of his temporarily gained certitudes:

> They are the divisions and inbalances
> of his whole concept, made weak by pity,
> flouting desire; they are— No ideas but
> in the facts.

The irony of the transformation of "No ideas but in things" to "No ideas but in the facts" must not go unnoticed.

But, as if to confute this seemingly rock-bottom defeatism, a new note enters through the prose of a letter whose writer, evidently a literary man, urges the poet "to submit to your own myths." The past, T.J. insists, is nothing apart from the present:

I have said that the artist is Ishmael. Call me Ishmael, says Melville in the very first line of *Moby Dick;* he is the wild ass of a man;— Ishmael means affliction. You see, I am always concerned with the present when I read the plaintive epitaphs in the American graveyard of literature and poetry . . ."

Perplexed by this advice, Section III reveals the poet impatiently turning upon himself in a bitter confessional:

> How strange you are, you idiot!
> So you think because the rose
> is red that you shall have the mastery?
> The rose is green and will bloom,
> overtopping your green, livid
> green when you shall no more speak, or
> taste, or even be. My whole life has
> hung too long upon a partial victory.

THE POEMS

But the poet, even as he wills to hold himself to particulars, cannot be so bound for "in the attic which is
desire," if I may borrow a phrase from an earlier poem, his
thoughts soar "to the magnificence of imagined delights"
and soon he is making a new poem. This poem, with its
curiously rugged quatrains (except stanza 2 which has
five lines), with their intertwining pattern of half-rime and
end-rime, and by eschewing end-stopped lines contrives
an exceptional and appropriate fluidity. The problem of
identity is considered, a theme which had been introduced
by the letter in part two as the question of the-past-in-
the-present, and the poet asks "Who is younger than I?"
The reply is quixotic: an optimism born of self-knowledge
tries to strangle a pessimism born of world-knowledge;
man's vitality and his unwilling recognition of the limits
of that vitality wage a clandestine and eternal inner war.

There follow some sketches of subterfuge and desperation, among them one of those swift tableaux of "personality" which Williams handles so deftly:

> Will you give me a baby? asked the young colored woman
> in a small voice standing naked by the bed. Refused
> she shrank into herself. She too refused. It makes me
> too nervous, she said, and pulled the covers round her.

Serving as contrast to the double negation of human potentiality effected by fear and caste is the opulent house
with the private herd, the swimming pool ("empty!"),
the orchids "like weeds, uncut, a tropic/heat while the
snow flies" as a special maid grooms the Pomeranians
"who sleep." But before the full effect of waste can be
felt in this swiftly itemized milieu of conspicuous con-

131

sumption, there is superimposed, montage-fashion, a short prose catalogue of the "goods and chattels" of one Cornelius Doremus, who died in 1800 appraised as worth $419.58½. The itemization of Doremus' meager effects serves as ironic counterpoint to the unused luxuries of the modern absentee landlord. The poet considers who is responsible for the "restriction of knowledge." Here "knowledge" is an inclusive symbol for goods, social goods, language, in short, the modes of human intercourse. He is unwilling to assign guilt to a special group although the university denies its raison d'etre and perpetuates the stasis. But there are others who "are also at fault because/ they do nothing."

The poet envies the men who run off to "other centers, direct—for clarity (if/they found it/) loveliness and authority in the world—/a sort of spring time/toward which their minds aspired" but which leaves the poet who cannot run off so, "ice-bound." The obvious allusions here would seem to be to Eliot (authority) and to Pound (the past).

A third accident, occurring at the Falls in 1875, is now described. A human body is found lodged between two logs overhanging the precipice. But the age of the miraculous is over. The poet is more and more confined to a recognition of the hideous industrial present: "the ravished park/torn by/the wild worker's children . . . ," a present which will more and more take possession of the poem in Book II:

> He thinks: their mouths eating and kissing,
> spitting and sucking, speaking; a
> partitype of five.

> He thinks: two eyes; nothing escapes them,
> neither the convolutions of the sexual orchid
> hedged by fern and honey smells, to
> the last hair of the consent of the dying.

The content of this sense-collecting spills itself before the poet's consciousness in its tawdry unsatisfactoriness: "pathetic souvenirs, a comb and nail-file in an imitation leather case—."

But the metamorphosis of the poet continues ("such is the mystery of his one two, one two"). He becomes one of the many: ". . . among the rest he drives/in his new car out to the suburbs, out/ . . . where the convent of the Little Sisters of/St. Ann pretends a mystery." Here are the blank, vulgar streets with which the poet must grapple and upon which he must beget his dream. And he rehearses, at the lowest level of brute fact, the data which this world offers him: "An incredible/clumsiness of address,/senseless rapes caught on hands and knees/scrubbing a greasy corridor . . . /Plaster saints, glass jewels/ and those apt paper flowers . . . have here/their forthright beauty," even the "things unmentionable/the sink with the waste farina in it and/lumps of rancid meat, milk-bottle tops: have here a still tranquillity and loveliness/Have here (in his thoughts) a complement tranquil and chaste."

The ordering process of the imagination is the term Williams rings on the "materialistic sadness" which Mr. Tyler accurately perceives as the tone of his interest in decay. This interest is implicit in the concept of death-in-life Williams shares with Yeats. The imagination, "a complement tranquil and chaste," while not triumphant

133

over decay has, at the least, an equi-valence as a category of value, or existence. This is central to Williams' position: he is not subscribing to the autonomy of art; he is not affirming the exclusive "reality" of *things;* he is saying, to the contrary, that while ideas (imagination, art, knowledge) are rooted in things ("No ideas but in things") they can, nevertheless, achieve an independent validity when "raised" by a willed act of creation.

Immediately consequent on these considerations, occurs the line "He shifts his change." The word "shift" refers us back to the doctor-poet (although there is no reference to the poet's "real" profession) in his car and also points to the sudden acceleration of the poem through the prose description of an earthquake. The abrupt shifting of the soliloquy back to narrative permits the poet to fuse into a new configuration the complex features of the poem, just as an earthquake, through violence, may re-order topography. The subterranean sources of thought, of myth, of speech (the subconscious is represented by "that moist chamber" created by the hedge of the Falls' torrent) are held up to the light in their prismatic mystery.

Paterson Book I leaves us, at the end, with a glimpse into that mystery ("thought clambers up,/snail-like, upon the wet rocks/hidden from sun and sight—/hedged in by the pouring torrent—/and has its birth and death there/ in that moist chamber . . ."). The poem itself represents "the myth/that holds up the rock, that holds up the water" and it "thrives there . . . in that moist cavern," where "inspiring terror" stands shrouded watching, in the din,

134

THE POEMS

Earth, the chatterer, father of all
speech . . .

. . . .

Paterson (*Book II*) the latest installment of Williams'
work-in-progress appeared in the summer of 1948 and
although it is too early for all the returns to be in, the
critical response is affirmative. Book II deals with the
modern replicas of "the elemental character of the place"
which was the subject of Book I. It exhibits an appropriate
drop in key. Indeed, the musical analogy for *Paterson's*
structure recommends itself even more powerfully after
a reading of Book II. Looking back to Book I from its
vantage point, one sees how skillfully the major themes
were established there as in a symphonic overture. In
effect, and to shift the metaphor for a moment, Book I
contains in embryo not only Book II but the others which
are to follow. Book II, "Sunday in the Park," in its narrower formal purpose suggests the first movement of a
symphony, although its prevalent mood of disenchantment suggests an andante or largo tempo throughout. It
requires less exegesis because of its evolutionary descent
from Book I.

Paterson, now signifying both the poet and the historic
shade of "the place," strolls in the Park, "female to the
city," and like a lover "instructs his thoughts" upon her
body. Walking about the rocky paths in the late spring
afternoon he sees about him only the deprived and cut-
off citizens, workers and their "wild children" whom the
elemental Falls had presaged in Book I. The "ugly legs
of the young girls," "the red arms of the men," the Negro

135

girls "their voices vagrant/their laughter wild, flagellant,"
all, all are

> Minds beaten thin
> by waste—among
>
> the working classes SOME sort
> of breakdown
> has occurred. . .

Only the young lovers lying "beneath the sun in frank
vulgarity," exposed to the public view, manage to achieve
a pathetic domestic dignity, a semblance of communion as

> their pitiful thoughts do meet
>
> in the flesh—surrounded
> by churring loves! Gay wings
> to bear them (in sleep)
>
> —their thoughts alight,
> away . . .

And still "the great beast" (Hamilton's term for the
people) comes to sun itself and seek its pleasure, "celebrating the varied Sundays of their loves." Behind the
memorable portraits—the man combing the new-washed
dog, the old Italian woman feeling the regenerative throb
of Spring, dancing, her skirts lifted, the bored lover asleep,
a beer bottle clutched in his hand, as his girl tries to rouse
him to desire,—one hears the rumble of the Falls, the
soft tread of the Indian feet which made the first paths
through this ground.

But the elemental character of the place is smothered
by the deformity of the present. How is Paterson, the in-
quiring philosopher, to decipher the meaning of this reduced world? Reviewing various items of frustration, he

sees an urgent necessity to change, to "invent." The cultural desert of the present cannot merely be abandoned; some mode of regeneration must be found. Those who are familiar with Williams' critical vocabulary will recognize how charged a word "invent" has become in it. "Invention" in Williams' earlier poetry dealt always with the art of verse, while now in Book II, introduced as a minor theme, it is a principle expanded to include all experience:

> Without invention nothing is well spaced,
> . . . unless the mind change, unless
> the stars are new measured, according
> to their relative positions, the
> line will not change, the necessity
> will not matriculate: . . .
> . . . the old will go on
> repeating itself with recurring
> deadliness: without invention
> nothing lies under the witch-hazel
> bush, the alder does not grow from among
> the hummocks margining the all
> but spent channel of the old swale,
> the small foot-prints of the mice under the overhanging
> tufts of bunch-grass will not
> appear: without invention the line
> will never again take on its ancient
> divisions when the word, a supple word,
> lived in it, crumbled now to chalk.

This plea is elaborated by a hint of the Evangelist's presence. We can hear him shouting somewhere in the park and later we find that he too urges invention through self-loss. Now we leave the drab dramatis personae who, nevertheless, have taken on a brilliant mythic clarity as they are etched in the hot sun of an afternoon's vision.

137

Just as the key word (if reduction to a "key" word is not a poor stratagem for exposing so complex a texture of meaning) of Book I was "divorce," so the key word of Book II is "blocked." It is the first word of the second section. And the poet, in his own person, adds sardonically "(Make a song out of that: concretely)." "The great beast" is blocked by the Church, by the pursuit of money, and by money's power when it is not pursued: "An orchestral dullness overlays their world." Into this dullness the voice of the old Evangelist "protesting—as though the world were his own" does not penetrate. The superb vigor of his testimony as he tells of his emigration to America, his acquisition of money, his happiness, "as happy as money could make me," only to end with the question "But did it make me GOOD?" is answered by his own thundering "NO."

> I couldn't eat, I couldn't
> sleep for thinking of my trouble so that

> when the Lord came to me the third time I was
> ready and I kneeled down before Him
> and said, Lord, do what you will with me!

> Give away your money, He said, and I
> will make you the richest man in the world!
> And I bowed my head and said to Him, Yea, Lord.
> . . .

> So I started to get rid of my money. It didn't take
> me long I can tell you! I threw it away with both
> hands. And I began to feel better. . . .

"Is this the only beauty here?" the judging poet asks. And he concludes:

> The beauty of holiness
> if this it be,
> if the only beauty
> visible in this place
> other than the view
> and a fresh budding tree.

But "the preacher, outnumbered, addresses/the leaves in the patient trees." No one heeds his exhortation and in the background, engraved with a delicate, elegiac grace is the sad image of

> The gentle Christ
> weed and worth
> wistfully forthright
>
> Weeps and is remembered
> remembered as of
> the open tomb

It is our descent from the sources of energy and vision once animating Western culture which Williams deplores. But, unlike some others of his contemporaries, Williams sees that this tragic descent cannot all be credited to a malevolent "scientific" present. Its roots are in the past as well. Thus, against the Evangelist's ringing witness, is put a bit obviously the ironic contrast of prose excerpts detailing the grandiose plans of Alexander Hamilton for creating a Federal manufactory in Paterson, a plan which failed, but whose imitation has successfully disinherited the "place" of its native vigor. In this category too are prose passages of an anti-usury, anti-credit content reminiscent of Ezra Pound's polemics on these subjects. Throughout this contretemps of giving and getting, of prayer and denial, the thread of pitiful self-analysis initiated by the woman writer in Book I continues. Now her letters become more demanding in her desire to communicate "not impersonally, but in the most personal ways," with the elder writer who keeps her off. She is "blocked" too, as are the others. The poet himself is blocked by the equivocal spectacle of the Falls and its branching river, "bride and father" in whose "composition and decomposition," mysterious and apparently contradictory principles of energy, he finds "despair."

Nevertheless, the third section firmly takes up the rich vein of hope enunciated by the Evangelist and ignored by "the great beast." It supports this new direction with the recapitulation of the plea for invention made earlier. This collaboration is first expressed in the terms of paradox:

> But Spring shall come and flowers will bloom
> and man must chatter of his doom. . .

> The descent beckons
>   as the ascent beckoned
>   Memory is a kind

> of accomplishment
>   a sort of renewal
>   even

> an initiation, since the spaces it opens are new
> places
> . . .

>   . . . A
> world lost,
>   a world unsuspected
>   beckons to new places

> and no whiteness (lost) is so white as the memory
> of whiteness.

Love begins to waken as night advances and the pouring water announces what we have lost and what we may find. The "story" thread now becomes explicit once more: "the great beast" dresses, must be out of the Park by nine, and Paterson, now in the guise of Faitoute, the giant, (the pun should be noted) rejects these puny modern replicas and strolls off. But the poet (only another aspect of the vast, multiple consciousness of Paterson) is bitterly disturbed by his inability to

> . . accomplish the inevitable
> poor, the invisible, thrashing, breeding
> . debased city

The malady is the malady of the modern industrial world. The city is

> . . . debased by the divorce from learning,
> its garbage on the curbs, its legislators
> under the garbage, uninstructed, incapable of
> self instruction.

And the "language" with which to divine this riddle still evades him.

> Only the thought of the stream comforts him,
> its terrifying plunge, inviting marriage—

But She (the river, a female principle) responds:

> Stones invent nothing, only a man invents.
> What answer the waterfall? . . .

Now all the persons of "Sunday in the Park" pass before the poet's vision and his thwarted desire for a

141

resolution of the conflicts they have raised within him causes his anger to mount. An ugly holocaust of deformity begins to blossom in his brain. A staccato torrent of contradictory injunctions from the falls, the river, and his own conscience pour in upon him. A voice advises:

> Be reconciled, poet, with your world, it is
> the only truth!

And "She" who has been crying "Marry us! Marry us!/ Or be dragged down./dragged under and lost," accuses the fleeing poet, "You have abandoned me!" Faitoute reestablishes himself as the dominant mask of the Paterson personality. The theme of love, sounded early in this section, is amplified. The poet resolves to "regain/the sunkissed summits of love!" even though the means involve a descent "to the screaming dregs." A fine lyric, set in the narrative as if being reviewed in the poet's mind after composition, seals the ritual, celebratory mood "On this most voluptuous night of the year." Now,

> The blood is still and indifferent, the face
> does not ache nor sweat soil nor the
> mouth thirst. Now love might enjoy its play
> and nothing disturb the full octave of its run.

The clear, grave music of this beautiful song gives way to the subjective refrain:

> Her belly. her belly is like a white cloud. a
> white cloud at evening. before the shuddering night!

Thus, at the very end of Book II, the climate for an act of consummation is evoked. One anticipates a possible renewal through the complex chemistry of love. But, as

142

if to confound prognostications, and adding an anti-climactic note of mockery, there is a postscript in the form of a six-page letter (begun earlier in the book) from the rejected woman. It is a rambling letter which in its prideless honesty is a moving exposition of one who has found no consummation, either through work or through love. The letter is written to Dr. P. (P. obviously Paterson, while "Dr." is a new accretion to the personality of the Paterson protagonist) and is full of biographical references to Williams' own history as, for example, that P. wishes to use the writer's letters in *Paterson* and that he has written on the necessities of the woman writer in an article on A.N. (Anais Nin).

These letters serve in a curious double agency. They have a part in the total design of *Paterson* similar to the anti-poetic "historical" prose-threads. But while the historical text documents the poetry, objectively, at the level of public life or society, the woman's acute yet distraught letters document the poetry subjectively, at the level of private life, in her case a losing revolt against society. In effect, Williams makes an ironic attack on himself through the medium of the barely disguised letters. This amounts to a kind of penance, as if the poet were confessing: Here in *Paterson* lie exposed the polar contraries of modern experience. On the one hand, there is the affirmation of art in the poetry; on the other, the mean inadequacies of conduct, in the letters. Who is to divine the abyss or construct modes of reconciliation?

We are left with this irresolute paradox at the end of Book II. Against the expectant gesture of the last lyric passage stands the harsh agony of the accusing letter.

143

Nothing has been consummated. Anything—or nothing—can happen. Williams is now at work on Book III, which, he earlier promised, "will seek a language to make them [the modern replicas] vocal." Meanwhile, the achievement of the first two books is considerable. Both texture and structure everywhere collaborate to one end: It is in the earth (things) that we must find and know our sources; it is the earth as material reality which fathers speech (ideas, imagination). Thus Williams' original assertion, "No ideas but in things," has become translated by the *very process* of the poem itself: the poem is the documentation of *how* ideas come from things. Beginning with a seemingly uncompromising materialism, the poem, in the end, arrives at an almost classical humanism. In *The Delineaments of the Giants* the poet by "a celebration, a taking up with the bare hands" has raised himself to the stature of the giants. For, disguised as "Mr. Paterson," as "I," as the very Falls themselves, he is the only sensibility in *Paterson* who knows his sources. Knowledge is the key to possession; possession the condition of relationship to a human whole. In so far, then, as the individual accepts and possesses his sources, both in the social world and also in the world he makes for himself out of that world, is he liberated to be truly human. Books I and II represent the initial critical discipline in the forging of that modern epic of man's eternal search for divinity which the whole of *Paterson* promises us.

All of Williams' recent poetry reveals his fidelity to the vows of his sacramental union with the "filthy Passaic" in the rococo "The Wanderer," a long poem in which he had attempted to define his role as poet thirty years before. It is a poem whose river symbolism foreshadows that of *Paterson* and may be thought of as nuclear to the later work. In it the timeless knowledge and flux of the river with its "vile breath of degradation" must first be embraced by the poet in a mystical marriage without which his own powers would be unfulfilled. Much of Williams' energy has been dedicated to tending the fruit of that consummation, one by which knowledge of evil becomes a postulate of self-knowledge. It is clear now that in *Paterson* Williams is attempting one of the most adventurous and passionate assaults upon the moral structure of the American grain which the poetic imagination in this country has yet conceived. Such a quest for self-knowledge implies a loosening and so *losing* of self, a casting-off, which in the most purely illumined terms of morality is discovery: ". . . and whosoever shall lose his life . . . shall save it."

II

THE PLAYS

IN WILLIAMS' POETRY THE DRAMATIC ELEMENT SO NOTICE-able in the poems of Eliot, for example, is almost entirely suppressed. But the tendency to suppress is gradual and derives, I think, from Williams' slowly developing aware-ness of what is proper to the various media which in-terest him. Proper, that is to say, not to any codified dis-tinction between dramatic verse for the stage or lyric verse to be read but, more organically, proper to his intentions. We have noticed the Browning influence in the implied dramatic structure of some early poems. Moreover, Wil-liams' earliest literary impulses moved ambivalently be-tween play-writing and poetry. While the poet appeared to conquer the playwright, Williams' need to *objectify* relationship (a primary source of drama) reasserted itself on and off with increasing intensity.

Williams' juvenilia in the drama are instructive. Like all beginnings, they tell much about his preoccupations and his shortcomings. In a rough way they are prophetic

146

not only of his development as a playwright but also as a poet, for the writer is a total personality of which playwright, poet, novelist, critic are, after all, only separate facets. *A September Afternoon,* written in 1909 while Williams was finishing a year's internship at the Nursery and Child's Hospital on San Juan Hill, in Hell's Kitchen, until just recently known as one of the worst slum districts in New York, is a one-act play, static in tone. It is placed in Fishkill-on-the-Hudson in the crucial year of 1776 when that area resounded to many skirmishes between the British and the native farmer-guerillas. The characters are Barney, an American boy of seventeen, and his sister, Marjory. Most of the action occurs off stage, a familiar failing in apprentice-playwriting.

What interests the young dramatist, however, is not the off-stage conflict between the British and the Independents, but the moral conflict between Barney and his sister, each standing for a segment of colonial opinion, and each illustrating the perennial recurrence of two kinds of "resistance" to circumstance. The conflict is pointed when Marjory challenges Barney's patriotism with: "What country? You're a lot of fools fighting over a cow and that's all . . . It's the fight only that draws you on." Barney hotly denies this, saying it is for those who will come after. To which Marjory replies: "They'll be just as big liars and stealers as they are now . . . lying and backbiting and grabbing for the most they can lay hand to and fearing each other worse than England or the Devil himself even." Later, Barney is wounded and dies.

The dialogue, while striving for realism, sounds as if the young playwright were reading Synge and the Irish

147

"folk" writers who, at the time, had considerable prestige. Speech cadences are more Irish than American. The rhythm and the inverted syntax of the following is illustrative: "For the love of God come home, you crazy boy! Come home! It's this we've been fearing the two weeks now they've been camping beyond the hills." The climax is anti-climactic and the motivation inadequate for us to sustain much sympathy for Barney's sacrifice. In short, the play is little better than a literary dramatized argument.

But it is Williams' impulse to examine the reality of the American revolutionary myth, and the relatively objective way in which the issue is joined by the representative and symbolic figures of brother and sister that is interesting. For the play was written before the flurry of excitement caused by Van Wyck Brooks' *Wine of the Puritans* (1909) had stimulated inquiries into the character of the American past.

In *Plums,* composed at about the same time, Williams examines the meaning of the revolutionary issue from another point of view, the point of view of the landowner whose intelligence and cultivation has brought prosperity and eminence to the Hudson valley and who, by aristocratic allegiances as well as self-interest, is with the British. The Yankees, represented by two plum-stealing soldiers, are shown as crass, marauding and unperceptive of the true quality of the land they would "free."

The fact that Williams dealt separately with these two aspects of the Revolutionary War shows the young playwright's insecurity in handling a moral conflict which, in effect, he admits to be a complex one. Instead of exposing

its facets to the light as would a more experienced dramatist and securing an *opposition* of several points of view,
and so a richer quality of drama, Williams, realizing his
technical limitations, isolates areas of the conflict and then
deals with them each in order. The conflicts, drawn so
directly, become oversimplified. What is valuable is Williams' early recognition of the plurality of attitudes which
the Revolution sucked into its destructive and liberating
fire.

. . . .

In *Sauerkraut to the Cultured,* subtitled "A Nieu Am-
sterdam Comedy," and which I take to follow *Plums,* Williams deals with a larger range of social values, although
on a scale of lesser heroism. The inquiry into American
mores is pushed even further back. The time is the summer of 1680 after the Dutch have lost the town. The play
opens with a conventional triangle outlined in a weak
blank verse by an English youth, Fred Pickel, who aspires
to win one of the conquered enemy's daughters, Lena Bach,
who is also sought by Karl Minnewit, a Dutch youth. As
in an Elizabethan prologue, Fred sketches the scene:

> At first the morning: we'll be occupied
> As is our custom with the things
> Habit has fitted to his back as cushions
> In an old chair.

This description adequately suggests the tone of the
piece, which is domestic, gentle, humorous and affectionate. Old Johan Friedrich Bach, Lena's father, exemplifies
all the solid, no-frippery burgher virtues which the young
English gentleman would batter down by gifts of roses.

The wooing, then, becomes the wooing of Lena's father as much as of Lena, and it is by the progress of Fred's graceful blandishments over the old man's habit, that we measure the progress of the courtship. The quality of the old man's personality deepens as Fred tries more and more to demonstrate the good will of the English and draw the family from its seclusion. Old Bach refuses his offers, saying:

. . You new ones in the city are so busy improving, that you never have time to learn, but I live by profession evenly. All your misery comes from mixing levels. As long as men keep to their levels all is happiness but if a man live at knee level and pretend to the chin level his end is fixed. I, sir, live a little above the knees.

In reality, it is old Bach who is the protagonist of the play. He loves his bells and talks of his "genius" with them. They are "solid" and not like the Englishmen's flutes. Now the struggle for Lena intensifies and Fred naïvely proposes to his rival an ingenious contest for Lena's hand. A new law requires that each citizen must place a beacon before his house on dark nights. The young man who devises a method satisfactory to old Bach gets Lena. Fred proposes a hickory post, curved into an elegant design and hung with a bronze lantern; Karl, a nail, with Bach adding, "a tin lantern." Bach rejects the post although Lena is for it, when suddenly Fred cries:

I cannot ask a man to pretend falsely to anything, neither will I agree to make my post less beautiful . . . Why sir you must change your life to fit my post . . .

Bach: What will you do?

Fred: It is all philosophically correct this time. First comes my new

lantern, then we'll change the front of the house to fit that,
then the inside to fit the outside, then the furniture to match
the walls, then will come clothes to match the furniture and
so on until all is raised to one level, that of my lantern.

Karl is crushed, while Lena is chagrined to think his
imagination has not risen to the challenge. Karl relin-
quishes Lena (against her secret desire) as to a better
man. But Lena produces a picture of a post which she has
directed Fred to draw for her and presents it to Karl, thus
signifying her rejection of Fred. The play ends with the
promise of a concert on the bells from old Bach and the
wedding on the morrow: ". . . we'll dissipate till half
past nine tonight if we burn three candles."

This odd little play, while lacking plot, movement or
suspense, is charming and warm. Old Bach is swiftly
developed in three short scenes and there is a nice balance
established between a Jonsonian "humours" character
and a seventeenth-century "manners" type. Bach's speech
is lively and robust. The chief significance of the play is
Bach's insistence on being "common," his resistance to
modish foreign influences, and the eventual triumph of
commonness as represented by the native Karl. The play is
an immature allegorical foreshadowing of the position
Williams was later to develop in his aesthetic—his championing of the local, the indigenous, the "common." It
underlines the kind of question which the young writer
felt compelled to ask himself. Like the previous plays,
Sauerkraut to the Cultured is a study in values. The conflict is not between kinds of *motivation*, but between fixed
standards of value. The battle is waged not in the realm

of psychology habitual to modern drama but rather in that of morality.

. . . .

A decade and a half later Williams was still thinking about the drama, even though no longer its practitioner. In an early version of *A Novelette* appears the following:

> Note! The conception of a lyric or tragic drama demands lyrics! Studies in language should precede that, the spontaneous (not natural conformations of language) as it is heard. Attempt to feel and then transcribe these lyrical languages in *Paterson*. The drama, the lyric drama (Lope de Vega) should be one expanded metaphor. Poetry demands a different material than prose. It uses another facet of the same fact; . . . Fact, but just before and just after the incident which prose (journalism) would select and by that, miss the significance poetry catches aslant!

This note reflects the way Williams' mind stubbornly refuses to relinquish a design once it has taken root and how, once rooted, it fuses with his other speculations. Everything, as happens with any genuine artist, flows together and enriches everything else.

It was at about this time that Williams was toying with the notion of a play about the beginnings of America, an aim probably springing from the nexus of research which had produced *In The American Grain* in 1925. There are some interesting manuscript materials which illuminate the growth of that notion into the *Libretto for An Opera on George Washington* published in *The New Caravan* in 1936. One of these is a one-act play, *Under the Stars*, about Washington and Lafayette. Lee, Washington's insubordinate general, had been reprimanded for misjudging the contest. Washington, in the midst of victory, has pangs of conscience for his treatment of the officer but Lafayette reassures him of its correctness. The talk is stilted and insecurely managed. What is significant in this exploratory sketch is the psychological emphasis: the conflict is developed *within* a single person by a dramatic opposition of various facets of his temperament. This represents a technical advance over Williams' earlier practice of assigning conflicting values to different characters in the play.

Another unpublished play, *The Battle of Brooklyn,* with an epigraph from *Hudibras* describing the rabble as the riders of the State, also appears to spring from Williams' revaluation of American history. The emphasis here is upon low characters—townsmen, servants, etc. While the conversation between Lady Gates and her serving maid is brittle, witty and on the side of Restoration bawdiness, the gentlemen, notably Washington and Stirling, do not come off so well. Their talk sounds like an exchange of eighteenth-century letters. However, the character of Washington is nuclear to Williams' later conception. Washington is apprehensive of the colonists' anger should the tide of battle run against them. He sees himself as the tool of "their diabolical determination to entail war upon my fellow subjects of America." It is hazardous to reconstruct the possible theme of the play as only one act appears to have been completed. Williams seems unsure of his intention for the first act does not succeed in establishing a direction.

At about this time Williams was trying his hand at various tasks in the theater. Cheaply got-up pink playbills in the U.B. Collection show him listed as Producer for The

Tyro Theatre Group, apparently a family-and-friends affair. Both Williams and Mrs. Williams appear among the actors. Most of the plays of this period were destroyed, including a Shavian comedy modelled on *Fanny's First Play* called *Frances For Freedom*. The MS for a one-act comedy, *Les Américaines or What Have You* is included in the U.B. Collection. The most significant effort of this period is not, properly speaking, a play at all in its completed form but an "opera." Nevertheless, its intention is dramatic although Williams finds he has to relinquish some aspects of traditional drama. The unpublished *Introduction to the George Washington Libretto* is important on several scores: it makes specific judgments about American Revolutionary history which Williams did not include in *In the American Grain;* it clarifies the technics of dramatic construction later used in *Trial Horse No. 1* and *A Dream of Love;* and it illustrates the radical analysis which Williams always makes of the form he happens to be using.

The purpose of such an opera, he writes, would be

To project the figure of George Washington across the panorama of American History so that it would galvanize us into a realization of what we are today . . .

A projection of this man of "powerful imagination" would require a tremendous music. Washington is seen as having created "an imaginary republic . . . pasted together a good deal out of shoddy to represent the thing we still endeavor to perfect . . ."

We can only create him in our own image. (Can't have him storming across the stage, singing arias). . . He cannot become a real figure then of his own day. He must be musically conceived, liberated from his own actions . . .

How to keep the recognizable features of an historical [?], his local significance, and still make him a fit figure for the universality which music can treat.

In a revision of this note, he adds: "With music the audience is liberated from following the mere plodding historicity of the event . . . It will look for the *meaning* . . ."

Wrestling with himself is characteristic of Williams' method. Often, as here, he puts the wrestling—that is to say, the creative-critical problem—into the thing he is constructing. This is not too different from the practice of Proust, Joyce and Virginia Woolf who also delineate an internal and discursive aesthetic in much of their writing. But Williams takes less pains to disguise the immediacy of the problem to the particular invention in which it is imbedded. This has certain limitations, the effect of which I suggest when discussing the *Great American Novel* and *A Novelette*.

The moment chosen in Washington's career is when he is going up for the Presidency, disliking it but

compelled to go, tragically, to serve again and against what odds . . . The plot is the destiny of a man in love with his fate in a distraught conglomerate of people bent on being themselves, whose word 'freedom' has infected him too.

Williams evaluates the scenes he has sketched:

Arnold's deception is a thrust at a part of his [Washington's] own self—he would have liked to live the kind of free life Arnold did. Then Newburgh where his aides plot to destroy Congress and he sees the liberty of action he craves in others bring them to degrada-

155

tion. Now rises in wrath and crushes Lee who disobeyed him at Monmouth. Fury unreasonable . . . The fury of his own life biting upon itself . . . This must be reported, not directly acted.

The catastrophe is seen as beginning with the inauguration of the first president who is eventually turned on by the mob and broken.

In a supplementary Section III, *Data, Notes,* Williams pointedly writes: "The second act introduces the real villain of the movement, Demos, in the person of the townsman (Gat). . . . At this period, rich as he [Washington] was the word which appeared most frequently in his diary was 'alone.' " Then, as if to draw together his own conflicts about the treatment, Williams summarizes:

The real theme, the music, is love right enough. It is a love music, a transference of a self love to the mob, to the common, to the people. . . . It is a love that rather than be thwarted enlarged itself to spread over a great area and to a great depth.

When these considerations were objectified it was into *The First President: Libretto for An Opera (and Ballet),* written in a stiff, archaic and deliberately anonymous blank verse. The emphasis is on effective theatric action, on crises in movement. Speech elements are comparatively scanty and read more like an outline of the action. The special genius of Washington's temper so clearly perceived in Williams' notes does not come through in the play. He has since learned much about what makes credible play-talk. Here, we see Washington in a series of vignettes which although unconnected manage to hold interest. It is possible that the right music could elucidate the "play" as a unit.

Whatever its limitations, *The First President* is interesting for its technical innovations for they demonstrate Williams' close study of the potentials of the stage, a study which was to bear its richest fruits twenty years later in *A Dream of Love*. Still, it falsifies Williams' stubborn insistence upon what he feels to be central to a *perception* of reality to discuss it merely as "technique." For his use of dream is at once a means to an end and an end-in-itself. The dream has of course had many exponents in twentieth-century writing. Among the best known are Joyce, Kafka, the Surrealists and the group sponsored in *transition*. I shall discuss Williams' dependence on Joyce in *The Great American Novel*, a dependence which Pound was quick to recognize. Qualitatively, Williams' use of the dream is different from Joyce's. Joyce appears to value the dream (especially in *Finnegans Wake*) as the most significant mode of reality, the mode which reforms, informs, and elucidates other aspects of the "real." Williams, on the other hand, conceives the dream as a *superior* form of reality, an "ideal" form, toward which "reality" strives. The full implications of this distinction emerge in Williams' most philosophically ambitious compositions to date: *Paterson*, Books I and II and *A Dream of Love*.

In *The First President*, Williams writes: "The properties are never very clear, existing rather as the state between waking and dream." At first, the dream would seem to have a therapeutic or cathartic function.

> Dreams of trials overcome
> Should clear away tomorrow's trials

Sustaining the dream atmosphere, the figures of Martha and George disappear without the lowering of a curtain.

157

Later in the opera the figure of Washington appears above the usual plane of action, feet hidden so that he appears to float "brooding over the action. The figure assumes also the function of a 'chorus.' The totality of the opera is, of course, impossible for the literary critic to judge. It would only be in circumjacence to the music which Williams conceives as *prior* to the opera that any final judgment could be made. Unfortunately, this music while projected by Georges Antheil, whose work Williams had championed in this country, was never composed.

. . . .

When Williams wrote his next plays some ten or twelve years later, he brought to the task not only the more refined ear of the poet who in *Paterson* is revealing the texture of American speech, but also the fuller grasp of *situation* and *event* which the writing of *White Mule* had yielded. Thus, when Williams began to explore the idea of a play with contemporary subject matter (for the first time abandoning his historical themes) he had a large fund of materials to draw into his design. As with almost all Williams' rough drafts, the notes and early versions of *Trial Horse No. 1* are helpful in seeing the growth of his own knowledge of his aims.

In a folder in the U.B. Collection labeled "Talk" one finds the raw materials for one of the one-act plays in *Trial Horse No. 1*. Bits of dialogue are noted on scraps of paper. There is a prescription blank with a key perception jotted down: ". . . Marriage is only a second cousin to love." In a version of *The Funnies*, there is one of those definitions of the form he is exploring which, as we have

158

seen, is habitual practice for Williams. Interestingly, he restates the approach of the George Washington opera: "The stage is of no importance except as a clue to the imagination . . ." But the addition is significant: Williams has shifted the center of responsibility from structure (in *The George Washington Libretto* the music was to do the work for the words) to audience, as active participant in the play:

The players do no more than to interpret and make apparent what the audience is experiencing, thinking, giving that release . . . for obviously it is the audience not what is on the stage, that is the primary work of the author's imagination—not the play which only shows them up.

One of the five drafts of *The Funnies* has the subtitle "A One Act Play in Several Scenes" and this suggests that the plays in *Trial Horse No. 1*, were originally conceived as separate one-act plays. Apparently the three prose plays depicting related milieus of suburban mediocrity were written first. Once Williams perceived that they had a related theme, the depiction of various kinds of love, he appears to have constructed the verse play which, in the final version of *Trial Horse No. 1* (published by New Directions in 1942) runs through the three prose plays and welds them into a finely soldered unit. The verse play is the thematic thread which not only gives continuity to the three plays with their three separate casts but, at the same time, supports and enriches the meaning.[1]

[1] After this explanation had been constructed, I received the following description of the composition of the play from Dr. Williams:

". . . I was at that time vaguely interested in a local 'little theatre' movement . . . But I soon realized that it was impossible for me

In the sketchy notes the poet and the producer are conceived of as a Chorus, the play to be "definitely *verse*, if possible poetry." The theme of the play is "ringing the changes in the idea of love." Later, there is a bold, pencilled note: "Insert cogent verses—, my own! As Shakespeare inserted songs (for) pause, recapitulation, emphasis!"

Williams' interest in Shakespeare, as we shall see, is a long-standing one. On the published title-page of *Trial Horse No. 1*, the epigraph is from Shakespeare: "Let me not to the marriage of true minds admit impediment . . ." About ten years earlier, in a note dated November 24, 1927 (in the U.B. Collection), Williams, reflecting on Shakespeare, had written:

The drama is the identification of the character with the man himself (Shakespeare and his sphere of knowledge, close to him). As it flares in himself the drama is completed and the back kick of it is the other characters, created as the reflex of the first, so the dramatist "lives" himself in his world. A poem is a soliloquy without the "living" in the world. So the dramatist "lives" the character . . .

In *Trial Horse No. 1* Williams uses "his sphere of knowledge, close to him," a knowledge of the variable quality

---

to write for any local group of this sort for the moment I became serious it got wholly beyond the actors . . .

Of course my chief interest as always where the theatre is concerned is the language, verse first of all if it can be swung. And so the theme grew. I wanted verse. I saw that ordinary verse was impossible. So I goaded myself to study a possible verse.

The final coalescing idea was to fix the bastards in their places by commonplace prose playlets, something to hold their *first* attention after which I would have my try at them with the intermediate verse which was my deepest concern."

and tone of "love" to create the "back-kick" of the characters in the prose-play. In the verse-play, by making the
protagonist a playwright he ingeniously transfers "the
man himself" to a visible plane, before the audience's eye,
and in the actual process of *creating* the back-kick. In
short, *Trial Horse No. 1* is a play, a comment on what a
play is, and a demonstration of how a play gets written.

One can say, then, that the prose scenes are to the verse
counter-play as "normal" love, the theme of the prose
plays, is to "abnormal" love, the theme of the verse play.
And since the verse play twines in and out of the action
of all three of the prose plays, the contrapuntal ratio persists.

What is most essential to note is that Williams contrives
that an event in the counter-play ("the discovery of this
love by the backer") "supplies the climax and catastrophe
of the play." In other words, the "play" as a totality, the
theme of which is "love—of a sort," is dependent for its
resolution on an action occurring in the counter-play alone.
This raises an interesting question. Is it sound to have
one climax for "Three completely unrelated scenes" and
a counter-play? If we bear in mind the structural relationship of the plot and subplot in Shakespearean drama,
this device seems not too ungrounded. Furthermore, if
we accept the play's structure as analogous to musical
structure, the single resolution of the contrapuntal themes
seems valid.

Williams' impetus in *Trial Horse No. 1*, comes from his
consideration of Shakespeare rather than from any other
single source. In describing the second prose play, he
writes: ". . . a young man and a young woman of high-

school age, comparable to the lovers of romance, are as-
sailed by the girl's father." Later, Hubert, the young poet-
playwright, says to Peter, his prospective backer:

> My purpose is
> to write for the stage such verse as never
> has been written heretofore.

Peter: I thought so.
         Better than the Bard of Avon?

Hubert: No, not better. Not at least the
         same—diluted down. A new conception, more suited to
             ourselves
         our times—which wants to use
         its brains.

They agree that modern audiences do not like verse in
plays, and Hubert adds:

> There is no verse, no new verse
> to write a play in. That's why. Invent it.

To this, Peter, the aesthetic, emotional and sexual opposite of Hubert, replies:

> This is the professional stage. When the
> faucet is turned on the water must run hot
> or cold as they want it.

In Act II, Hubert makes even clearer the exploratory
and tentative nature of his writing:

Hubert: There can never be
         a play worth listening to except in verse.

         .   .   .   .

> The words must carry a special meaning,
> a special dramatic structure of their
> own. What is the dramatic structure

162

as it occurs in words? Verse. That
is the drama of words—words, in love,
hot words, copulating, drinking, running—
Bleeding!

.   .   .   .

You see no one knows what it is.
They've never heard invention on
the stage. No one knows what poetry
should be today. It should be the
audience itself, come out of itself
and standing in its own eyes, leaning
within the opening of its own ears,
hearing itself breathe, seeing itself
in the action—lifted by poetry to
a world it never knew, a world it has
always longed for and may enter for a
few precious moments never to be known
in prose. The audience is the play.

The playwright (the "playwright" can be thought of as
a multiple projection of both Hubert and Dr. Williams)
then announces that the second play, is, like the first, in
prose. There is a quizzical humor in this turn-about-face
of methods. For it is only in the counter-play that we get
the verse and not in Hubert's three short plays where we
might reasonably expect to find it. It is at this point, no
doubt, that the single figure of the playwright splits in
two, as if playwright 1 (Williams) were saying to playwright 2 (Hubert) "Look about you young man and listen.
Your intentions: excellent! But it's not so hard as you
think to write verse for a play. See! I'm doing it." Or,
again, it may be a device by means of which Williams says
to the audience "Take your choice; or, measuring both

163

against Hubert's invisible ideal, don't you think both are usable?"

Between Act II and Act III there is no connecting tissue. But the third prose play, *Talk*, ends only to precipitate a continued argument between Hubert and Peter regarding their antagonistic values. As if to anticipate the objections of the conventional theater-goer whom he represents, although raised to the *n*th power, Peter argues:

> What is there here?
> No heat, no lifting of the scene
> no tension—no romance!
>
> . . .
>
> In the theatre to kill you've got
> to kill! With a hammer if need be . . .

Hubert defends his position by saying he has used the method of a trial horse to "approach" his aesthetic:

> . . . it should project
> above the coarseness of the materials—
> something else, in the words themselves
> tragic without vulgarity. Seen!
> in the mind! the mind itself—today,
> without firearms and other claptrap
> in its own tragic situation. We can't
> do this at once but must restudy
> The means.

And there it rests until the action of the play itself takes over. But Williams' open-handed, if artful, gestures of intimacy with the audience must not be taken as coy "asides." Hubert and Peter are not merely commentators on the action but participants as well. Hubert is the hero or protagonist; Peter the villain or antagonist. They are never merely threads on which the scenes are strung but, rather, the very agents of the single crisis and denouement which integrates the plot.

Now, a play after all may flow from its characters. Posit the people and the action should follow. We saw in the early plays that imperfect realization of character was one of Williams' weaknesses. In *Trial Horse No. 1* Williams has an ambitious program. But the very nature of his structure effects a limitation in characterization. He has four sets of characters to explore: three sets in the prose plays and one in the verse counter-play. Still, Williams has stated some of the characters swiftly and brilliantly. In *Serafina*, the first prose play, the character of the "boy-friend" emerges during his brief presence gemlike, humorous and profoundly American. Yet, Serafina herself, the Polish-American light-of-love, apart from a few uproariously bawdy lines, seems over-much like the stock "sensitive" harlot who has been too much with us of late.

Williams' failure to develop motivation fully enough shows up most damagingly in the climax of each prose play. In the second play, *The Funnies*, the curtain falls on the Lesbian, Miss Breen, who has come to inspect the farm Ann's people have for sale, embracing Ann (whom she has seen for the first time) and exclaiming, "It's all right, darling, I'll take care of you." Although such a relationship may be implicit in the character of Miss Breen as it interacts with the character of Ann, it is precipitated too baldly for credibility.

Similarly, in *Talk* where the characters are more successfully developed, the curtain goes down on a sleepy child, who, wandering into the kitchen, points at the old Doc whom her mother is feverishly kissing, and cries, "Daddy!" One grins, of course, but somewhat as one would at the black-out ending of a comedy skit. It is doubtful whether this is the response Williams sought.

Still, many of the characters are solid, three-dimensional and highly individualized conceptions. Clara, the handsome, wine-drinking suburban housewife is really a small masterpiece of poignancy and despair. All of the farm people in *The Funnies,* with the exception of the "heavy" father, Pete, are convincing. The comic interludes in the park, devoted to the younger generation, are unbelievably funny in their crude American fellowship. And in the verse play Peter, the homosexual backer, is exceedingly well-drawn in his seismographic fluctuations between sensibility and a boorish cruelty.

The important thing about *Trial Horse No. 1,* is the extraordinary sense it conveys of movement as apart from plot. Things are always happening and the fluidity of the action is charged, so to speak, by the language. Williams' ear has always been agile and delicate. It tells here in his genius for cadences that are at once generically American, and, at the same time, highly individualized. Clara, the reluctant and disorganized mother, speaks in a style that separates her effectively from the other lower-class characters whom, culturally, she tops by perhaps a rung. Into her pitiful, incessant talk which she herself dimly senses has pathological roots, she throws, innocently enough, a note of social inquiry which colors everything in her personal chaos.

"Believe it or not! I haven't got that much mother love in my whole carcass. What do you suppose is the matter with me? I just haven't got it. . . . I'm trying to do my job as a sweet mother and it's killing me. I'm telling you, killing me. If I quit this whole mess of having children and sent it to hell and gone out of my sight, I'd be a better woman, and that's the truth."

And the Doc who follows her emotionally, while his intellectual refining of the situation plays an invisible counterpoint to the tense, wine-flushed mood that Clara has set up between them, speaks a crisp, clipped language culturally remote from Clara's. The talk grows curiously more searching, more centripetal to each speaker, until by the end of the vinous confessional both Clara and the Doc are lost in Chekhovian self-immolation. It is a failure of personality which the Doc at least intellectually recognizes:

"Talk, talk, talk! Everything runs out finally into talk . . . And pretty soon we'll all be dead forever and never have opened our eyes wide once wide, that is, to see what actually—starved as we live because we never, never, never, took a chance among the five or six thousand or million people of our small personal world to know them actually and individually—what actually the creature in the next bin is doing or feeling . . ."

"To know them actually and individually—what actually the creature in the next bin is doing or feeling," is the urgent motive unifying *Trial Horse No. 1*. For in a series of vignettes as diverse as the individuals who compose them—from the industrial proletariat in *Serafina*, the up-state New York farm family in *The Funnies*, the lower middle-class housewife in *Talk*, the classless

professionals, Doc and Hubert, to the socialite Peter—
Williams is doing just that. In *Trial Horse No. 1* it is the
fatal blocking of this need that stunts the flower of love—
fatal because the self is so inwardly lost it does not even
wish to understand the nature of its "love."

An exciting aspect of this organization of curiosity is the
felicity with which the counter-play impinges upon and
alters the action of the prose plays. The effect is a per-
plexing but heightened sense of reality such as a mirror-
reflected-within-a-mirror-reflected-within-a-mirror perspective might produce. Yet the inner unity by which
these many loves are integrated is one flowing as much
from Williams' essentially ironic compassion for all his
people, as from the carefully engineered and novel outlines of his framework. While, as Hubert says, the mind's
eye is good enough to see *Trial Horse* in, it would fulfill
Williams' hope (see his synopsis and stage directions) and
test the validity of his theories, to see and hear it where
it rightfully belongs—on the stage.

. . . .

On the whole, *Trial Horse No. 1* should be thought of as
preliminary to Williams' recently published *A Dream of
Love* (1948), a play which he ranks in importance with
the epic poem *Paterson* and which, in a sense, is even
closer to his own spiritual biography. It is difficult to reconstruct the genesis of *A Dream of Love*. Notes in the
U.B. Collection dated from 4/45 through 7/9/45 are written on separate sheets as well as on prescription blanks and
comprise "Details," corrections, scraps of conversation,
as well as a first sketch which roughly outlines the struc-

ture of the play. *A Dream of Love* was originally planned as *A Dream of Love—or Josephine Thinks Her Own. Sextette.* Josephine is the colored maid who apparently was first conceived as more central to the action. The title suggests a thematic continuity from the "many loves" motif of *Trial Horse No. 1.*

The dream, both as device and as value, had interested Williams as far back as the *George Washington Libretto.* Love, it is clear, has now usurped the dominant focus of interest. *A Dream of Love* would seem to be Williams' paradoxical definition of the fusion of these themes: love as a dream of love, and dream as a love of dream. Since this paradox is central to the play as well as to aspects of *Paterson* I have only touched on in Chapter I, it is worth gathering Williams' notes on the dream element from the various trial drafts of the play. He writes "The dream has to be 'natural' except to indicate that it is a dream after which the listeners are to forget that temporarily—until rudely awakened." Later, he adds ". . . real as in a dream, everything, so real we are terrified and convinced." And perhaps to be connected with this: "The situation, as in a dream, becomes unbearable to her but to the listeners also. Will he get it told before the end?—a double tension."

From the beginning the three main characters, the Doctor, the Other Woman, and Myra, the doctor's wife, appear to be fairly distinct. Obviously, the contest is to be over the dream of love which each holds up to himself. One version has the doctor reading a poem which is clearly intended to set the tone:

> The region of doubt and dream
> round which our lives are welded

the unfathomable fundus
of our guilt—assume measurable
proportions in our doing

The doctor's dream is to be realized at the end in one version through the vision of HER (the Other Woman) naked, in the shower (of rippling light). ". . . She has said YES. They have completed the act. This is the vision he has sought. Now he is completely happy. The play has been accomplished." Williams had not worked out the meaning of this "accomplishment" to his own satisfaction for he asks: "The husband (wins) if that is what it is called." He is uncertain as to how to dispose of the wife. "She to cling or reject him. Which is the crisis of the play."

A revealing note deals with Myra's attempt to find out from the Other Woman what was said the day her husband died. "(Blocked when she tries to find out WHAT was said . . . But what is REVEALED, what actually took place—in his [mind?] to call it that, What is *real*. What is the real for *her:* love. If that is lost then everything is lost." It is clear (and we are fortunate to have all the clues to his intention that these fragmentary notes provide), that Williams was wrestling with a conception reminiscent of the theme of *The Tempest*. He approaches his answer even before he writes the play. It is to be a *dream* of love.

This, plainly, is a deepening of the psychological pluralism implicit in Williams' notion of "many loves" into a more radical philosophical inquiry into the nature of "reality." The old motif of the dream as "ideal" and the newer concern with the nature of "love" welds together the horned paradox of the title. An ironic note in the first version says: "The end is happy. She possesses him dead." But the irony is not merely for Myra, but for all of us with our many dreams of love, possessed only *in* dream.

Williams' inquiry into Shakespeare, as we have seen, always pursues a double direction: he wishes to get at the psychological weight of the plays, but he is equally interested in the psychological *interaction* between the created object and the creating being. This has little to do with "biography" in the vulgar sense. In some unpublished notes in the U.B. Collection, dated November 15 [?], 1927, he writes:

"When he (Shakespeare) speaks of fools he is one; when of kings he is one, doubly so in misfortune. He is a woman, a pimp, a Prince Hal. Such a man is a prime borrower and standardizer—no inventor. He lives because he sinks back, does not go forward, sinks back into the mass . . . Everything written is subjective, King Lear, Hamlet, and objective when it is written. But there is no question which objects have the greatest firmness on the page and from that in the imagination: It is those characters which come in a well-settled form at its height of creation. It is the nine months of creative effort (extending over a century) which invents them. Then a Shakespeare, not burdened with knowledge as such, who loosely comes into the inheritance and with a nascent brain makes and eats the fruit."

This early note illuminates the clearly autobiographical cast of *A Dream of Love*. The protagonist is a middle-aged doctor; the setting is a suburban community that might be Rutherford; the doctor, miraculously enough, like Williams, even writes poetry. What then? "Everything written is subjective . . . and objective when it is written." By keeping so close to the facts of his own mode of life, Williams is merely trying to rescue for himself the kind of "commonness" of experience which for Shakespeare existed in another way in the vast public domain of drama and letters on which he squatted so casually and "anonymously" and from which he spun his uniquer majesties. The modern stage poet has not "these characters which come in a well-settled form at its height of creation . . ." nor can he "loosely come into the inheritance . . ." By drawing quite casually on what is close to his experience Williams seeks to simplify the task of manipulating *this* reality into the imagined "reality" which is his meaning. By choosing characters and situations which strongly suggest the career of his own biography, Williams is being "autobiographical" no more and no less than the artist who paints a picture on the brown paper sack his wife has emptied of onions.

I do not wish to suggest that Williams was unaware of the risks he ran by choosing such close-to-home dramatis personae, any more than Byron was unaware of the risks of autobiography when he penned his ingenuous disclaimer to the first cantos of *Childe Harolde*. For even the most casual, ready-to-hand-selection which an artist makes is connected with his inner necessities. It is possible to accept the objectivity of Williams' play and yet to see that by staying anchored to his domestic moorings he is liberating himself of his own psychic burdens. But, after all, what is important for the reader is not what the creative act does for the artist, although that is always a fascinating inquiry, but rather what, once created, it does for him.

In its completed version *A Dream of Love* is composed

of three acts divided into eight scenes. The epigraph is a passage from John Addington Symonds *The Greek Poets* describing Menelaus abandoned in his home by Helen. In Williams' play it is the man who leaves the marriage bed. But the essential relationship is deeply comparable for Myra and for Menelaus:

"Yes, in his longing after her who is beyond the sea, a phantom will seem to rule the house . . . But dreams that glide in sleep with sorrow visit him, conveying a vain joy; for vain it is, when one hath seemed to see good things, and lo, escaping through the hands, the vision flies apace on wings that follow on the paths of sleep."

The first scene of *A Dream of Love* swiftly establishes the relationship between Dr. Thurber and his attractive blond wife, Myra. They have been married for some time; the children are "away," perhaps married. The Thurbers are ambivalent in their feeling for one another. Dr. Thurber chafes at his professional responsibilities and puts his writing of poetry first. He loves Myra, but not exclusively, and is unperceptive about her needs. Myra loves the Doctor, admires his poetry but feels insecure and, at times, rejected. She resents the fact that she is ungifted, that the Doctor has had other women during their marriage and that she is so dependent on him for her emotional satisfactions. The tone of their talk is frank and affectionate but while Myra is capable of a sprightly wit, there is an undercurrent of reproach in almost everything she says. She reminds the Doctor that it is their anniversary and asks if he remembers what he said the day he proposed.

Myra: You said, "Love you? Hell no. I want to marry you."

Doc: I don't believe I said that.

Myra: Then I asked you, "Why do you want to marry me?" and you said "To love you, I suppose."

Doc: Was I that intelligent—in those days? It must have been real passion.

In Scene 2 we follow the Doc to the home of the Randalls, a young suburban couple who are his patients. Dotty Randall, dark and attractive, is typing a play for the Doc. But this is a mere pretext for the Doc's visit and while Cliff, the salesman husband, is fixing drinks, they arrange a rendezvous for the next day, thinking he is unaware of their relationship. But as soon as Dr. Thurber leaves, Cliff accuses Dotty of being in love with him and learns that she is "bored to death." She insists she is going off to the city, next day, to "talk" with the Doctor. Cliff, rather pathetically, tries to approach her and she rejects him contemptuously. By the end of the first act, then, the lines of conflict have been clearly drawn. The marital tensions in both households have been demonstrated and the direction of the subsequent involvements has been established.

The opening scene of Act II discloses the kitchen of the Thurber household with Josephine, the colored maid, and the aggressive, intellectual-looking milkman discussing Dr. Thurber's death of a heart attack in the hotel room he had engaged with Mrs. Randall. The milkman argues: "She's a good-looking lay, why the hell couldn't he stay home?" The maid defends the doctor and says the thing was unlike him. The milkman expostulates:

To take a woman to a hotel that wasn't his wife? Sure it could be any man at all—those things happen every day. I will admit you don't have to drop dead in bed with her. That was bad—in fact that ended the doc. But it shouldn't have happened, that's what I'm trying to tell you. And it wouldn't have happened except that he was just an amateur, poor guy . . .

As he talks, quite without rancor toward the Doc, we learn that he has a crush on Myra and intends to marry her. Josephine is incredulous and reminds him he has a wife. The milkman breezily replies: "I got enough on her to blow her into the middle of the Pacific Ocean any time I want to spring it." He talks of his business ambitions (he is now the owner of a small milk-route) and his belief that being married to Myra would be advantageous to him. When he leaves Myra comes out of the pot closet dirty and tired. She has seen no one since the day of the accident. She sits dejectedly at the bottom of the back stairs and it is there that the figure of Dr. Thurber may "possibly" be made out. Various apparitions also occur in this space later in the play. The voice of Dr. Thurber is heard speaking one of his poems: "a dream we dreamed/a little false/ of love/and of desire, we two. We have slaved/we have dug/we have bought an old rug/we batter at our unsatisfactory brilliance." This will be recognized as a reworking of a section of Williams' "Perpetuum Mobile: The City."

On the common-sense level of the action, talk goes on between Myra and Josephine, but yet with a suggestion that some breath of the doctor's presence has come to Myra. Mrs. Randall comes to the door and Myra goes back to the pot closet. The Voice of Dr. Thurber is heard again to speak: "As the rain falls/so does/your love/bathe every/ open/object of the world . . ." The passage, an elegiac comment on the Doctor's feeling for Mrs. Randall, is adapted from one of Williams' finest lyrics, "Rain," which is discussed under *Poems*. Ironically, neither of the two women (who are now both vis-à-vis in the kitchen) are aware of the Voice. Death is the interloper and the rivals are closer to one another than either one is to the dead man.

Mrs. Randall, compassionate for Myra's sorrow and guilty for her share in it, asks to be forgiven. Her character is an enlargement and deepening of that of the neurotic suburban housewife in *Trial Horse No. 1*, just as Doctor Thurber may be considered a full-length portrait of the physician sketched there. She too loves the Doctor because "I needed him and because he knew, without me saying more, how much I needed him. Because he is a writer, a writer about things like that—a poet." Both Mrs. Randall and her prototype are symbolic types of modern disorder: confused, valueless women cast in pre-shrunk, de-valued housewive's roles which they do not wish to play.

Myra will meet Mrs. Randall on only one level: she asks her with a blunt intensity how often she has slept with her husband and what was said about her. Like many women in love she wishes to possess the entirety of her role in the loved one's eyes. The need to see herself from the point of view of both "the other woman" and of her husband as lover of the other woman is a pathetic attempt to grasp the imaginative totality of what she "means." It is her way of trying to fix the boundaries of identity or personality, in short, of her own "reality." But there is a bitterness in Myra's probing, a masochism in her attempts to learn whether Mrs. Randall was going to have a child, whether the lovers planned to marry, and so on. All through this contretemps Myra seems coarser and less sensitive than "the other woman." Yet one feels it is a forced response to the death of Dr. Thurber, a death which, by its circumstances, has deprived her not only of love, but even of the idea of love.

There is a violent scene for Myra tries to keep Mrs. Randall from going. When she finally breaks away, Myra's phobia prevents her from following and she throws pots and pans about in a fury of frustration. It is clear she is becoming mad. Josephine indicates she won't be able to keep coming in. Myra asks her to come just once more. As Josephine leaves, Myra stands listening while the curtain descends on the confused and mocking domesticity of the kitchen.

The first scene of the third act follows the frightened but loyal Josephine in her visit to a faith-healer, Mrs. Hardy. This episode is well written, the idiom rich, colorful, and without quaintness, as it captures the cadences of Negro speech, but it is difficult to see its contribution to the total movement of the play. It is true that Josephine prays for her mistress' cure and is given a charm to help her. One may, of course, connect Myra's eventual return to normalcy with Josephine's prayers. But even such an explanation seems forced. This scene, included in early versions of the play (in the U.B. collection), and cut from the penultimate version, has now been restored. Apparently, Williams intended it to support the other "supernatural" manifestations (the Voice, apparitions, etc.). The reason it is not integrated with this matrix of the "supernatural" is that Josephine's actions are in the order of magic, whereas the other manifestations are in the order of psychological symbolism. Williams would be true to his original impulse about this scene if he were to drop it from any future acting version.

Fortunately for the dynamics of *A Dream of Love*, the following scene is sufficiently intense in its pace to re-establish the play in its proper orbit of movement. In the kitchen the same evening we find the ceiling absent and the stage lighted as in a dream. Myra is asleep on a cot when Dr. Thurber enters, tries to get food and casually remarks "Come on, get on the job here. I'm dead." The possibilities for humor here lie dangerously adjacent to the enveloping tragic texture. The milkman comes and goes silently, symbolically functioning as Myra's protector and suitor.

As Dr. Thurber speaks one of his own love poems, Williams introduces a daring theatric device: In the darkened recess of the stair-well is revealed the nude figure of a woman, which only the doctor sees, for it is *his* dream of love, before it as suddenly disappears. This device might be compared with the famous scene in *A Winter's Tale* where Hermione's living body, at first thought to be a statue, is revealed in the niche to Leontes' astonished eyes. Hermione, too, is a dream of love, but come true. Ironically, Myra is now loving toward her husband (as in her "real" life personality) and there occurs a strange, brilliant conversation between them which is clearly intended to be the chief "action" of this scene.

The talk summarizes, portrays, and *is* the conflict between husband and wife. And this conflict supersedes the individualized dramatic opposition of the two and becomes the conflict between Everyman and Everywoman, a tragic conflict of which the polar antagonisms are the human need for communion and the impregnable isolation of the individual soul. The doctor makes a superb attempt to plead his own view of this dilemma:

A man must protect his price, his integrity as a man as best as he is able, by whatever invention he is able to cook up out of his brain or belly as the case may be, a woman of some sort out of his imagination. Oh, it doesn't have to be a woman but she's the generic type: It's a woman—even if it's a mathematical formula for relativity, even more so in that case—but a woman. A woman out of his imagination to match the best. All right, a poem . . .

Myra, with a supremely damning lack of understanding, says: "Is that all?" Thurber, still carried by his own magnificent rhetoric, adds: "Then a man, of his own powers, small as they are, for once possesses his imagination completely—grabs it with both hands—he is made! or lost, I've forgotten which . . ."

Myra, from her cot, luxuriously continues her inquiry into her husband's actions before his death, saying "Oh, it is so marvellous to feel again." This clue to the essentially parasitic nature of her love is not underlined. The doctor probes his spiritual biography as the milkman sits protectively beside Myra, a coarse contrast to the tortured explorations of his rival. Dr. Thurber speaks with a passionate honesty of his boyhood and adolescence, its confusions and agonies. During this bitter confessional, Myra sleeps, again reaffirming their lack of rapport. She awakes and soon reverts to her prying questions. Dr. Thurber, angered, replies: "One thing about sex, you're never so happy as when you're rid of it . . . Every man is like me . . . I'm run of the farm, dull average . . .

That's my pride . . . Hellishly proud that I'm just the core of the onion—nothing at all. That's just what makes me so right . . ."

These crucial lines, recalling as they do the Gyntian definition of personality, connect with Williams' anti-metaphysical bias. He is against systems, "philosophies" not because they are systems but because they are the derivatory rather than the primary perceptions or "constructs" of experience; they "drag [s] at the heels of terror." It would be careless to equate this position with "primitivism." Williams' position does not push him into an advocacy of action for blind action's sake. It is action as catharsis which "lets a man rest at last." And rest, as this discarded passage from an earlier version of the play indicates, is the condition for creation. Action, then, far from being an anarch, is the *modus* of an ultimate order, peace, integration.

But Myra does not see this. She is intent on putting together the broken picture-puzzle of her image of "love." When she demands more knowledge of James's affair, he tells her he took Mrs. Randall "to renew our love, burn the old nest and emerge transcendent, aflame—for you!" With an obscure cruelty Myra tries to force him into the recognition that he is dead. She wants him to look in the mirror but James refuses. She demands to know "what you promised this woman before you dropped dead in bed with her?" And she insists he must speak honestly, "that I may forgive you if I can, and if I cannot, let you go out of my mind and out of my life forever . . ." James defiantly replies:

. . . the details are of no interest. So what? I live with you. I live from you. I am you. We are married. I do what I please . . . All my life I've been saying, Hello, my darling and Goodbye! the anodic opening and the cathodic schluss, the best moments of a lifetime—all yours!

Myra, persistent, asks why his profession couldn't have stopped him if his "love" for her could not. And Dr. James replies: "Life and death. That's the burden of my profession. What's there to learn in that? I am a man." Thwarted, Myra damns him and is answered by blinding lightning, thunder, and wind. Scene 3 is a superposition on the old setting of a few crude props suggesting a hotel bedroom and picked out by a strong light. In the illuminated area are the Doctor and Mrs. Randall. In the shadows of the stage sit the butcher boy, Josephine, the milkman, and Myra, alone, watching.

The lovers are drinking and the doctor urges the woman to undress, but she implores that he continue talking. He talks "patiently," about the universities, about the sonneteers, about the surrealists, of whom Mrs. Randall asks: "Don't you approve of them?" To which Thurber replies in Joycean fashion:

Approve of them, my dear girl? I *have* them. So have you, so have we all of us. The surrealists without grandmère or grandpère! Do you believe it? You a mother? all transported to dream. Do you pillow me? And nothing is left to the poet but the restricted pathetic world—into which we cannot be translated— . . . Come on, let's go home.

At this point, Myra, now a disinterested spectator, calls to him: "How can you be so thoughtlessly indifferent, so

181

cruel?" for Mrs. Randall is now visibly excited and has begun to undress.

The connection of this talk with Williams' often-expressed views is too obvious to require comment. But Myra's changed relationship to the action must be seen as elucidating the role of the spectator in the creative process: when Myra can imaginatively participate in her husband's life through the kind of vision brought by art, then she becomes disinterested—in the best sense of the word—and suspends judgment. She can even identify with the woman whom in "real" life she hates. As Doctor Thurber, at Mrs. Randall's request, continues his impassioned comparisons of the poetry of the Greeks and of his own time, she suddenly offers herself in words reminiscent of Molly Bloom's concluding paen of affirmation in *Ulysses*, crying, "Yes, now. Yes, yes, yes, yes, yes!" Thurber embraces her, her dress falls from her shoulder, while the others, with the exception of Myra who indifferently pares her toe-nails echo "Yes, yes . . ." which changes into machine-gun firing increasing in intensity.

As Mrs. Randall utters her final "yes," there is darkness pierced by flashes of light and the figure of a woman appears in the back-stairs naked, bathed in flashes of descending light as if in an illuminated shower-bath. Everybody mills about until there is a final explosion and the nude figure disappears. The milkman, seemingly wounded, falls on Myra's bed while she, in a Red Cross cap, tends him. When she kisses him and tells him he's not hurt, he shamefacedly disappears. Then Myra lies down and after thunder and lightning there is darkness and quiet. As at the beginning of Act II, Myra is in bed, alone, sleeping.

Dawn, when "reality" asserts its sway, is automatically making everything seem "normal" again. Groaning, Dr. Thurber comes from a corner, saying he is wounded in the heart. Where else? As he avows his love for Myra, "You were marvellous. You always gave a guy a chance," she replies that she forgives and loves him. As a rooster crows and the stage gets light, he staggers into the house to "go to bed, to our bed." Myra, at first unable to conquer her phobia about entering the house, follows. When the telephone rings we hear her explaining to a patient that the doctor is dead. From this moment on, she is clearly "normal" again. She washes herself at the sink. We hear the clatter of milk-bottles being deposited at the back door. A ray of sunlight enters the room. Myra casually walks through the swinging doors into her house and the re-possession of her "personality."

Myra's reintegration emphasizes the fragility of the dream which love has been to her. Her easy acceptance of the now demonstrated "reality," and the rebound we sense she will make (perhaps with the milkman to aid her), reflects a common view of the parasitic nature of woman's love, its deflection at *any* level of excellence by whatever man happens to be so fixed on his own destiny that she is assimilated, as it were, into the orbit of his personality. Myra's survival, her recovery from madness, is based as well on another sort of parasitism. As Williams wrote in a note for the first draft: "She possesses him, *dead*." It is the possession that counts for Myra, not the quality of the relationship. Crudely stated, the dead are dead, the living go on living—in all the complexities of desire which staying *alive* entail. Williams' employment of a dead man

183

as protagonist for a view of life is a brilliantly ironic trans-
position of the hope suggested by Ibsen's "epilogue,"
When We Dead Awaken, a play written at the age of
seventy, and bearing a striking similarity of theme to *A
Dream of Love.*

A Dream of Love crystallizes various problems and
themes in Williams' work which, up to 1946, had been
held in solution. The autobiographic elements are as clear
as are those of Ibsen in his self-portrait as Solness in
The Master-Builder or as Rubek, the sculptor, in *When
We Dead Awaken.* Williams has merely taken less trouble
to maintain the fiction that all the characters are fictitious.
This apparently casual self-revelation flows from his belief that the poet is every man although not, it should be
emphasized, Everyman. Thus, we can say of Dr. Thurber
what Ibsen said of Brand, the preacher, that he could as
well have been a musician or artist. For, like the artist or
the clergyman, the doctor too stands in an exceptional relationship to life and death and to the dream of love which
invades and evades man's heart.

The acting possibilities of *A Dream of Love* are limited
not so much by its use of dream-fantasy mechanics, for
even the commercial theater has ventured to exploit the
dream, but rather by its relatively simple scheme of action,
and by the *nature* of its talk, rather than its talkiness. For
contrary to popular impression, a great many plays we
find "good theater" are talky. But Williams' talk is compressed, elliptical and nuggetory, distilled, at the age of
sixty-two, from the total burden of his experience. It is
talk we understand better if we have some prior knowledge
of his other writings.

On the other hand, the symbolic elements in *A Dream of Love* are well objectified in the action, and if there is any flaw in the conception of the characters it is that they are not given a conventional "motivation" to establish their behavior. For example, the man-of-action milkman who early in the play declares his intention to marry Myra seems somewhat conveniently motivated. Yet it is important to remember that, like characters' sudden deaths in the novels of E. M. Forster, Williams doesn't really care about a naturalistic pattern of "character development" here, that his scheme is more like that of Ibsen's symbolic expressionism in *When We Dead Awaken.* From this viewpoint it becomes clear that Williams, like Ibsen, wishes to create a conflict in values rather than a conflict of personalities. This would account for the relatively sketchy outlines of some of the characters in both plays. Still, Myra and the Doctor come through superbly both as individuals and as symbols of larger classes of experience. It is their conflict, after all, which is the crucial one in the dull arena of marriage, as well as in the more shimmering dreams of love which inevitably accompany it. But it is possible that *A Dream of Love* will never be seen on the stage where it belongs for as Williams had noted some years earlier: "The nearer you go to truth the more dangerous your witness becomes—till it can not be told except under special rule and guard, as in a court. He who would use it carelessly or openly—is likely to be driven from the field."

That the "special rule and guard" selected for this high undertaking should have been that of the theater is not surprising. For the dramatic mode, it now becomes clear, was the logical end-product of Williams' long concern with spoken language as the materials of his art. Now the poet is no longer content with the creation of accurate speech representations as "portraits" but has moved, instead, into the natural sphere of language in action—dialogue. The theater, traditionally, has been the most objective medium for the resolution of such interests. Perhaps the richest possibility for the stripping of the verbal "object" to its essentials, to itself, lies ideally in the externalizing form of the drama.

III

THE NOVELS AND SHORT STORIES

THE LOGIC OF WILLIAMS' ALLEGIANCE TO THE QUEST FOR A
knowledge of localism, for a defining of the American
grain, has compelled in his fiction a restriction to American materials. The notable exception to this is his first
novel, *A Voyage to Pagany*. While its subject-matter is
ostensibly Europe, the Old World, it is, in reality, an assessment of that world through the eyes of an American,
its hero, and thus, in effect, an assessment of America too.
The Jamesian pattern of New World meets Old has in
Williams' novel a similar function. While this encounter
does not always change the two worlds, it nevertheless
mutually illuminates their two systems of value. And with
Williams (seemingly the last writer in the world to compare on *technical* grounds with James) the result, as in
James, is a judgment of America, a judgment perhaps as
ambivalent as James's although disguised by a more visible affection.

The years 1920–23, as I have indicated in my discussion

of *Contact*, were dedicated by Williams to a reconsideration of the various aesthetic points of view with which it seemed possible for a writer to identify himself. His editing of *Contact* must have sharpened the focus for such revaluation and, indeed, the discussions of policy in the five issues of that periodical reveal an awareness of the choices and, at the same time, an almost fanatical resistance to the contemporary pressures toward aesthetic conformity. The nexus of belief and value from which Williams' fiction has sprung is precisely the same nexus from which his poems, plays and criticism derive.

Perhaps the best measure of Williams' particular development of the concept of "the local" would be to fix its relationship to other formulations of the "American" problem in the arts during his time. The decade 1915–25 (roughly) while witness to a large exodus of writers and artists from the United States to other countries, at the same time, and perhaps for the same reasons, marked an attempt to create an "American" culture. This impulse was crudely nationalistic in many of its manifestations. It could be seen, for example, in the blatant "new localism" of Lindsay dedicated to the wish that smaller American communities might be enabled to survive by creating their own arts and crafts. The regional poetry of Sandburg sentimentalized in heroic terms the achievement of the pioneers and industrial leaders of the West. Robert Coady, in "The Soil," "a magazine of art," sought for an American art in the immediate and familiar. Coady tried, naïvely, no doubt, to find a native and popular aesthetic for America by drawing on photography, engineering, sports, the dime novel, etc., for his materials.

Perhaps the most sophisticated attempt to define the American task in letters was to be found in the pages of *The Seven Arts* which had on its editorial board writers like Waldo Frank, Van Wyck Brooks, and Randolph Bourne who, at distinct levels of intellect and outlook, were all similarly engaged in evaluating the American scene, its past and its future. Bourne's dissident, brilliant, and querulous anti-imperialist, anti-war stand differed sharply from the increasingly conservative, nationalistic orientation of the former expatriate Brooks. The quest for the Grail in each instance is pursued in the spirit not of the Grail but of the man who seeks it.

It is reasonable to assume that Williams could not have been unaffected by the powerful stream of investigation and, more dangerously, *wish,* represented by this search for the meaning of American experience. The significance of his own search is, as I have suggested, defined by his greater integrity of purpose, his sharper assessment of the problem. In 1928 Gorham Munson could say when comparing Williams' interest in American materials with that of his contemporaries, that "Williams differs . . . in that he has observed the limitations of his program and thereby kept it pure, he has confined himself to the strictly aesthetic problems of choice of subject-matter and the fashion of perceiving and handling it." [1] *Contact* had set forth a program for American writing which stressed the necessity for contact between "words and the locality which breeds them, in this case America." The distance between this kind of localism and that of the mid-western regionalists

[1] See *Destinations: A Canvass.* Chapter IX, William Carlos Williams: A United States Poet.

is, of course, radical. The former stems from a recognition of the relationship between experience and the modes by which it is ordered; that is to say, it recognizes the problem of technique and craft. The latter emphasizes merely the authenticity of the "local" as subject matter; it is essentially disinterested in form.

However sound Williams' formulation of his aesthetic in the early '20's may have been, the gap between his theory of fiction and his practice of it was nevertheless wide. Williams' first sustained fictional effort, *The Great American Novel*, published by the expatriate American Robert McAlmon at his Three Mountains Press in Paris, is a confused and confusing work, its impulse alternating between aesthetic argument and novelizing. This double agency of the novel as its own representation and its own critique is peculiar to the twentieth-century novel. We see it in Proust, in Gide, in Joyce and, quite distractedly, in the later Virginia Woolf. The act of writing becomes, along with what is being written about, the subject of the novelist's study. The *how* becomes inextricably entangled with the *what*. In *The Great American Novel* Williams never successfully *involves* the aesthetic with the "story" (what there is of it!) as do Proust and Joyce, and with lesser success, Mrs. Woolf.

Throughout *The Great American Novel*, Williams sits in judgment on his own performance. He is actor, producer, spectator, and playwright, the four persons of this "self" (the novelist) perpetually quarreling with one another. Quite characteristically, he writes of his writing: "It is Joyce with a difference." (Joyce had described *Ulysses* as "History with a difference.") He goes on to say in self-derogation: "The difference being greater opacity, less erudition, reduced power of perception."

The novel opens in a foggy September with the writer asking where to begin. It ends (Chapter XIX) ten months later with the rain coming down. This somewhat spurious circle is, I think, meant as a comment on Williams' sense of a failure of achievement. The fog and the rain signify his mood of perplexity at the beginning, his frustration at the abandonment of the enterprise at the end. In between, there has been some sprightly writing, fragmentary in its presentation of content, but with a recurrence of themes which suggests a "story" although, in truth, it never gets told. The problem stated in the first chapter, similar to the problem of Bernard in Mrs. Woolf's *The Waves*, "Yet if there is to be a novel one must begin somewhere," is never solved. Many false starts are made and rejected. The writer decides first to make himself into a story. Soon a third person narrative sequence appears but the biographical content is transparent. A doctor is going home in a fog from a meeting of the Mosquito Extermination Commission. He enters the bedroom where his wife lies in bed. "He smiled and she, from long practice, began to read him, progressing rapidly until she said: 'You can't fool me.'

"He became very angry but understood at once that she had penetrated his mystery, that she knew he was stealing in order to write words."

The next chapter takes up a new theme, consisting of revolutions around the motif "I'm new." There is the new baby, the new dynamo, etc., all speedily, accurately, and musically reported in a prose which cannot be paraphrased

adequately because of its compression. Suddenly, as if
to confront this aggressive newness, there are introduced
some aspects of the anti-poetic—the legless cripple, the
feeding dragon-fly excreting, "the little sound of this stuff
striking the earth could not be heard with its true poetic
force. Lost. Lost in a complicated world." Still, the grotesque, the deformed, although they are recognized in experience, do not yield the clue as to where the artist begins.

The first two chapters are concerned with content—
where to begin. From Chapter III on, the would-be novelist becomes increasingly concerned with style. Let us pretend, says the writer, that Joyce and Rimbaud have taught
us nothing. Joyce "has in some measure liberated words,
freed them from their proper uses. He has to a great
measure destroyed what is known as 'literature.' For me
as an American it is his only important service." [2] Soon
the writer is reminding himself ". . . Everything no matter
what it is must be revaluated . . . What are you trying
to say in this chapter? And what of your quest of THE
word?" His reply to this rhetorical question involves a
theory of communication: "First, let the words be free . . .
They are words. They will have their way." They do so in
an amusing parody of "romantic" writing describing the
attachment of a little runabout for a big truck. The question is now: What then is a novel? Various answers to
this are rejected, including Dadaism, and modern German

---

[2] Williams' references to Joyce are rather cold. His estimate of
Joyce was to change considerably later. One suspects that Williams
was so much impressed with Joyce at this time that, quite unconsciously, he had to resist him. See his later essay on Joyce in *An
Exagmination of James Joyce* first published in 1929.

poetry ("such a lot of things mixed together under one title").

Later, the "I'm new" motif of Chapter II is picked up again and expanded by the method of association into a "new world," Columbus' *Nuevo Mundo* motif. This leads to a consideration of the Indians, the fanatical terror and suppressed but domineering sexuality of Mormonism, and the low estate into which the Nuevo Mundo has fallen. The exploration of other contemporary features of the new world is continued in the description of a hysterectomy, symbolizing the new anti-romantic reduction of sex, an episode which leads to a consideration of "the history of women."

The writer then decides that the American background is America. "If there is to be a new world Europe must not invade us." Williams answers Vachel Lindsay's "America needs the flamboyant to save her soul" with the argument "America tries to satisfy this need in strange and often uncalculated ways . . ."

The imagination will not down. If it is not a dance, a song, it becomes an outcry, a protest. If it is not flamboyance it becomes deformity; if it is not art, it becomes crime. Men and women cannot be content more than children with the facts of a humdrum life— the imagination must adorn and exaggerate life, must give it splendor and grotesqueness, beauty and infinite depth.

A series of bright little vignettes, some only a paragraph long, exemplify the process of this creative energy. The old woman longing for the sea, the comely girl who leaves school, the little boys of nine planning tortures for their sisters' imaginary seducers, and other aspects of American "energy" past and present. There is a relation between past and present value:

The danger is in forgetting that the good of the past is the same good of the present. That the power that lives then lives today. That we too possess it. That true beauty is in good work and that no matter how good work comes it is good when it possesses power over self. Europe's enemy is the past. Our enemy is Europe . . . Everything we do must be a repetition of the past with a difference . . .

Chapter XVIII, a memorable chapter about a Cumberland mountain mother, is written in a guide-book style, which by its anonymity builds up into considerable emotional power. The mountain woman untouched by modern habits is seen as the "typical" American. The portrait of Livy, looking down at her first baby, as if it were "a holy thing" and saying, "I ain't a-goin' to whip him. He ain't never agoin' to need it, for he won't get no meanness if I don't learn him none," is magnificent.

Opposed to this nostalgic idyll are scraps of success-story clichés, travel-book excerpts, advertisements, petitions, etc., to suggest the feel of America somewhat as Joyce collected Dublin street-car transfers and racing forms to give him the feel of Dublin "dirty and dear."

The close of *The Great American Novel* sounds a note of crass modernity: a factory owner explains in an elaborate rationale of his venal motives that his product is not inferior. The incident, presented without comment, suggests how little we have to start with. The novel as a whole is a confession of inadequacy, an inadequacy faced up to by the novelist. The ironic title underscores the paradox. One agrees with Gorham Munson that Williams "never gets the novel under way . . . though he writes a flexible, fibrous prose."

The prose norms about which Williams' style fluctuated indicate knowledge of the possibilities but an insecurity in controlling them. The basic indecision as to what the subject shall be is caused not by a dearth of material but by an overabundance of it. The dilemma is *where* to fix value, for selection of data in itself implies value. Williams' failure to solve this dilemma, however, need not lead one to Munson's conclusion that "It is the situation of the Primitive." As a matter of fact, the true Primitive,[3] if such an abstraction means anything even as an abstraction, has no confusions about value. He not only rejects, but rejects *in favor of*. He is usually, like the true Traditionalist, didactic and secure in the exclusiveness of his system, even if his position implies a seeming rejection of systems. Munson later recognizes the inadequacy of the tag for he adds that one cannot "coop" Williams up as a primitive. The *post hoc* critic has the fortunate perspective of seeing *The Great American Novel* as a trial-

[3] It occurs to me that the term "anarchist" as employed by Herbert Read in *Poetry and Anarchism* might more justly be applied to Williams' position. Indeed, Williams' general ideological stand is remarkably similar to that of Read's.

On Read's resemblance to Williams' or *vice versa* (I doubt that there is a question of influence either way) the following passage is illuminating: ". . . there is nothing I so instinctively avoid as a static system of ideas. I realize that form, pattern, order are essential aspects of existence; but in themselves they are the attributes of death. To make life, to insure progress, to create interest and vividness, it is necessary to break form, to distort pattern, to change the nature of our civilization. In order to create it is necessary to destroy; and the agent of destruction in society is the poet." H. Read, *Poetry and Anarchism*, p. 15.

and-error investigation of the nature of the novel in our times. The stable, almost classically clear point of view to be seen in *First Act* is perhaps the reward of Williams' early agonizing over the form and substance of the novel. Had there been no inquiry, there might have been no achievement. Although unsuccessful as a novel, *The Great American Novel* might have carried real weight had it appeared as the "Notebook" or the "Diary" of the writer.

. . . . .

During the next five years Williams was coming to terms with the dubieties behind the choppy organization of *The Great American Novel*. The shape of this resolution was expressed in the title of his new novel *Voyage to Pagany*. In 1927, perhaps during the novel's composition or revision, there are among Williams' notes in the U.B. Collection the following remarks on novel styles:

But the "plain" novel style—Anderson, Hecht, Bodenheim is even worse. It is that they are unobservant and thoughtless of the things (too intent on the people and places and close stench) unbased on any solid conception that affects the style to make it direct—clarity. . . . The defect of . . . the just past novel . . . is that they have made a virtue of the philosophy and understanding of ordinary and stupid people as if there were some virtue in it. Whereas the book must be the discovery (among such people, if so it be) of an elevated theme . . . and they (the realistic figures) are subject to it . . .

A *Voyage to Pagany* published in 1928 and dedicated to "the best of us all, my old friend Ezra Pound," rejects the "plain" novel style, the depiction of "stupid people," and the "philosophy" of stupid people as well. For Williams' great novel of "ordinary" people, the book which was to be "the discovery (among such people . . .) of an ele-

196

vated theme . . ." was not to be written until a decade
had passed, a decade which was to bring with it profound
and radical alterations and derangements in the structure
of American society. In *A Voyage to Pagany*, then, written
in the yeasty post World-War I period when Americans
with and without money were invading the Europe from
which they had expelled the more brutal invaders, the
temper of one American's pilgrimage to the Old World is
made the measure of the gulf between the two societies.
The nature of the traveller and the journey itself are such
that the people involved cannot be "stupid" or "ordinary."
Significantly, the protagonist returns to that Europe which
earlier was the "enemy."

The section-titles elaborate the theme: Outward
Bound, At the Ancient Springs of Purity and of Plenty, and
The Return. Dr. Evans, a practicing suburban physician,
wishing to see the ocean once again "as he felt it still to
be, home of the wild gods in exile," sets sail for France in
1924 at the crucial age of forty, wishing he would never
have to practice medicine again so that he could give all
his time to writing although he "was a good first-line doctor." As France looms before him, he exclaims: "Now I
am come home to old Pagany." We know then that Evans'
is the mood of the exile returning to his rightful home
and heritage.

But as the narrative proceeds, reality intrudes new notes
into the first joy of his homecoming. The people seen from
the boat train look poverty-stricken and lost. "And their
poverty, this loss he began to blame on the death of the
gods. And they starve, they starve, not because there is
no food but because there is no one to give it to them
any more." Still his American humor, a love of the "anti-

poetic," perhaps, catches him short, acting as balance
wheel to the "romantic" imagination.

In Paris for the third time, Evans searches for its meaning, as in one chapter of *In the American Grain* Williams
in his own person had searched for that meaning. "Paris
Again" is particularly fine for Evans' childhood memories
of the city as they play against the present: "Good God,
Paris—he remembered how he had hated it; just an opportunity to shed the nerves, the cast-off international
malady, like the crutches at Lourdes." The frustration of
this search "was that he had to discard so much to get
at what he wanted that he never arrived anywhere . . ."
Soon Evans' old friend, the expatriate American Jack
Murray, gets into the narrative to complicate the possibility of Evans' eventual solution. The analytical passages with their continual qualifications, their incessant
concern with putting a value on relationships, are reminiscent in cadence and tone of Henry James. Evans is concerned to define the nature of his affection for Jack. The
nuances of love and the alienation imposed upon the
expression of it by his recognition of Jack's homosexuality
is beautifully handled in a prose with the true Jamesian
ring, altered by the more forthright colloquialism of latter-
day Americans. Evans wonders:

How the devil do you love a man anyway? . . . Evans loved his
friend, as a section of life where *he* was too weak to get at it, too
shy, too superstitious, too stately reverential.
He loved his younger friend for the bold style of his look at life . . .
Jack struck at the false and, in the thicket of good where it lay, it
perished—along with a number of other things. But when Jack
ignorantly had smitten, he Evans freely could breathe.

It is especially the disposition and the quality of the adjectives and adverbs the unusual "too stately reverential," where the adjectival "stately" almost has the function of an adverb, and the inverted adverbial emphasis of a phrase like "Evans freely could breathe," which suggest Jamesian practice in this section.

But if Dev Evans has difficulty in defining his feeling toward his friend, the difficulty is compounded by the complexity of his feeling for his own sister. Bess, who has lived in Europe for some time on a small income, paradoxically plays the double role of confidante and conscience to Dev. There are subtly stated overtones, too, of an almost wifely concern in Bess's tart castigations. Her opposition to Dev's values serve as domestically sober foil to his more extravagant claims for personality. Bess says:

"You think you are attempting something for America and for the world, you and your literary friends—your artistic friends. You rather look down on the politician and us poor tongue-tied mortals . . .
"You think we have no moral purpose?"

But soon the actuality of Paris begins to impinge upon these speculations and Dev is caught up in responding to places and faces. Places, even when they are contemporary, are seen in terms of art. But the artifacts of social congress like the Dôme, for example, are also seen in terms of their own inner psychological structure. Later, the themes of renewal of association, of self-examination, of social adventurousness, are interrelated. There is Dev's consciousness of Jack's watching his explorations, his awareness that he may not be showing up too well in Jack's cynical and worldly-wise eyes; the rounds of the night-clubs, the American girl's liquored caresses toward which Dev feels only "What? What?," the wind-up of all the tangled tensions in the fight with Jack walking home.

We learn that Dev has a rendezvous with an American girl, Lou, for whom the European trip has been arranged. The lovers meet in Carcassone where they are subtly depressed by the age and cold of the place. The thoughts of the pair turn toward the past, Evans being especially bitter toward himself. What Evans really would have liked was the total abandonment of self "with no end in view" like that "day the kids couldn't catch him at hare and hounds, that phenomenally successful day when he had kept them baffled all the afternoon . . . running, hiding, showing himself, and so on, hour after hour, running on. So, desperately scattered, he had remained still." Invaded by the cold, and feeling their separateness, the lovers decide to flee Carcassone for Marseilles.

The potentiality for conflict in the slowly kindling affair is already apparent at Villefranche, where Lou's interests (she had been an ardent tennis player and "through that means she had found her friends, formed her athletic opinions concerning life and built up her small talk") assert themselves. But at the Villa St. Denis, Lou appears to succumb to a setting which represents a challenge to her own values. And this giving up of herself corresponds to her physical invasion by love. "She melted, melted, melted under his delighted warming love which was an extraordinary south to her—until she was nearly freed from everything that had been America."

But soon the ominous periscope of a submarine invades

the idyllic sea outside the lovers' window (the sea of their love) and this alien note foreshadows a changed relationship between them. One day Lou announces that she has met a rich Englishman who has proposed and that she is leaving. Dev, although he had sensed she might go, is not prepared for the terms of her going, and is jealous. During their last night Lou offers to marry him. She tries to clarify her own motivation, her lack of understanding for "literary" people and "all this talk of art and writing." She wants to marry a man who has "a place." Dev is conscious only of a lack of feeling. "His design seemed frivolous beside the warm surge of Lou's realistic impulses." And the episode ends; the bachelor aesthete is saved from the icy plunge of marriage. "The next day they left the place, together, for decency's sake."

Thus begins section two, with Dev left free to search for communion and sustenance "At the Ancient Springs of Purity and Plenty." Lou's desertion has stripped Dev to his essential nature:

He had not known he would be so utterly indifferent to his loss . . . It is impossible to live— But impossible; therefore the arts have authenticity . . . Just to go, that's all—to turn into a steam engine with eyes . . . Insane to lose her, insane to keep her . . . Now, never dropping back to feeling, he was all eyes. The world existed in his eyes, recognized itself ecstatically there. This then was real . . . Elsewhere, everywhere he saw reality split, creviced, multiplied.

This passage sets the tone of the Italian section which reads like an inspired travel book. The reduction of experience to the piercing X-ray vision of the visual imagination is central to an understanding of Williams' prose and poetry, for the sense-data of the artist knows no division of purpose. When one remembers Milton's blindness, Wordsworth's color-blindness, one must recognize the conditioning role of sensory apparatus in the texture of the aesthetic experience. Williams as artist, like his protagonist, Dev, can at times become a greedy, omnivorous, optical sponge. But what the intellect does in liberating the content of the sponge is the measure of the gap between the *given* and the *made*. Thus, for example, the view of Genoa at night precipitates a vision of the sources of art:

Night. Not even an animal. The uselessness of all things froze his heart. All art is terror; one makes in the night . . . He saw all knowledge vanishing into the apex of a hollow cave—spinning off. Philosophic solitude—a dear delight. But that is philosophy. Alone is not philosophy; it is despair.

The term of emptiness had come upon him, the terror of no form, the poet's ache, and he pressed harder against the stone wall.

What then is art? . . . it is nothing but a form of the night . . .

It begins at the fingernails—it is there we see and begin within anguish, the fingers which annoy us being always in our sight. We pick at them. Or we make, to extend their length . . .

In the day Dev tries to gather to himself the excellences of an old world, and the descriptions of the Arno, of Florence take on an impassioned concentration of language that is close to poetry. Dev cuts through tradition and the sacrosanct to make independent evaluations of the forms and objects he encounters. Dev's search, a search for meaning presented in the artist's terms, is, in reality, the Faustian search over again. The ups and downs of Dev's approaches and glimpses of self-knowledge are seen in the many-faceted mirror of Europe.

Wishing to protect his anonymous, traveller's mood, Dev leaves for Vienna but on the train glimpses a girl who, one senses, will soon invade this neutrality. Williams' philosophic naturalism is revealed in the next section. A totally different mode of evaluating the world is forced upon Dev by the very brute data of that world itself: "When Evans arrived in the Austrian capital on the last day of March 1924, six years after Versailles, he found Vienna still showing marked traces of a reduced condition. . . . Everything seemed let down. He was impressed by a sense of desolation." The tone of Evans' response changes markedly. In Italy he had expressed little interest in the externals of Italian society, its politics, habits, etc. In Vienna Evans' purpose molds his mood: "Evans— had come to Vienna, as do so many doctors from the States, to observe new methods, to check up on his diagnostic technique and to prepare himself for adventures in his profession . . ."

Soon, we recognize that Evans' motivation as physician is similar to his motivation as artist. The search for meaning, clarity, value in each discipline comes from the inner nature of the *unspecialized* moral man. Evans' admiration for Knobloch, the tuberculosis specialist who pays for his experimental clinic out of his own pocket, and for the other professors, persuades him that

There was a strong sense of the priest in all these men, a priest presiding over a world of the maimed, living in the hospital, pondering and dreaming— . . . There was no feeling but the presence of the truth. It hurt an American. . . . In America we save men, without too much curiosity. Here they are lustful for knowledge, for completeness of living. These priests of beauty save men, but keep aloof.

203

I know of no better writing on such subjects than the scenes in which Williams records Dev's impressions of the hospital, the lectures, the demonstrations, and the patients. Even the syphilis of Vienna seems better to Dev than the "caponized athlete" of America. The trouble was America was raw, not primitive.

Through Miss Black (the girl seen on the train), a self-expatriated American, Williams projects a point of view which in reality is one aspect of Dev's conflict, but pushed to its farthest implications. For this reason Grace Black remains shadowy. Even her speech has a curious essay-like generality of tone. She is merely the brilliant stalking-horse for some questions which Williams wishes the protagonist to face. These questions revolve around the necessity for aristocracy, and it is a Jamesian touch that Williams should make the exponent of this position an American.

In the growing attachment between Dev and Grace Black, their attitudes toward America become the essential conflict. But Dev is leaving soon and she offers herself to him. In a magnificent chapter set in the old Imperial Riding Academy the particular flavor of this love affair is overtly dramatized before the parting lovers' eyes as they witness the exercising of the Imperial Arab horses. Grace, in the beautiful, rather literary diction which Williams allots her, sums it up:

"Is it not strange that everything we have for each other, animal, perfect and aristocratic, so strange to our society and training, that thing that makes us indispensable to each other that no one but an American can understand as we understand it with the same longing that we have had, you and I, what we call "love" has been evoked before us now, by these glorious beasts; . . . Here we have reached the climax of our minute . . ."

Later, Grace explains the quality in Dev's personality which offends her:

"You like Americans, thoughtless Polacks, Italians, Wops, not too much of them—because they do not matter too much, they do not cause you any serious concern. But fine people should not cause you any strain; they do though . . . You are not at ease with them as an aristocrat should be . . . That is why you now want to run to America where there are no really fine people—or they are buried, voiceless, lost—which amounts to the same thing, lost to sense, to understanding—and cut off from the ground . . ."

And Dev in the honesty of his nature, an honesty he later regrets when the sense of her loss comes over him, replies: ". . . I do not run from fineness, but small doses of it suffice. I soon tire. I feel a real need for the vulgar . . . Fineness, too much of it, narcotizes me."

Dev, escaping to the mountains, the mountains he sees from the train with the science of a paleontologist who can reconstruct a lost species from a few teeth and a skull bone, feels the fast-fading memory of Grace taking along with it the content of the pain. "To lose the pain, we lose memory itself until there is nothing more. Nothing should be forgotten, yet we must forget." Subtly, the movement of the train dramatizes the fluidity of memory and Grace's "reality" begins to melt.

Back in France, Bess takes over. For Bess, like Grace, is a projection of one aspect of Dev's complex sensibility. The sister-brother symbolism for objectifying what is essentially an inner conflict is successfully managed. Dev sees Bess' wish to keep him in France as a wish to domesticate

him for herself. He thinks "Always a woman tricks you—
and it's always the one you don't think is going to do it." But
Bess is insistent, and her plea has a strange wisdom. Like
Grace, her speech suggests an impassioned and impersonal
rhetoric difficult to credit to a particular woman. She is
really voicing one claim of Dev's conscience, the classic
claim on the over-sensitive American, owned up to by the
whole voluntary pattern of Henry James's self-exile.

"You and I have got to do something with ourselves. Americans. I
want to do some good with myself. Oh good, Dev, in the French
sense, the moral sense. To use well what we have, that's all. We are
incurably Americans, you and I, but we can help each other—if we
will. That offers us our only hope; to make a beginning, to make
something useful out of that country where there's no honor left but
a starved, thin lying one— . . . We've got to live with honor—
not the way we treated your precious Indians, Dev, but like a
Frenchman to whom France means something."

But Dev refuses to stay, Bess to go. There are nuances of
a kind of spiritual incest between the two. Bess, as one
aspect of Dev's personality, is trying to vanquish and
seduce the other strains to which he is loyal.

The last chapter of A Voyage to Pagany, "Off to the
New World," hints that through the process of frustration and pain, Dev has arrived at a new evaluation of
America. What that evaluation is is not directly stated. But
the final calm suggested by the description of the ship
in home waters, in spite of an undercurrent of melancholy, points to the possibility of a new achievement to
be wrested from an America freshly seen.

As the reader no doubt has remarked, A Voyage to
Pagany points to a close autobiographic orientation. The

hero like Williams, is a physician and a writer. The style of his responses to Europe are in the style we should expect of Williams. It is one that is personal, intense and unorthodox. Dev's radical departures from traditional estimates of Europe's wealth of art are based on the fullest erudition. Dev knows what he is rejecting and why he is revaluing. Indeed, *A Voyage to Pagany* perhaps more than any other single work of Williams should effect a revision of the "primitive" label. Throughout the European adventure Dev makes complex and crucial moral choices. In the end, the anchorage of his morality is an unsmug acceptance of his *difference* as an American, and his critical use of this difference for judging *both* America and Europe.

The tenor of Dev's relationship with women underlines the quality of this morality. Lou is rejected for she represents the crass, unselfconscious aspect of America which Dev would reject; Grace is lost because, although an American, she stresses an aspect of Europe, its diminished aristocracy of spirit, which Dev admires but sees he cannot *use* as artist; and Bess is turned down even though, unlike the others, she does perceive the quality of European living which might salvage the American artist from the dreary morass of his country's culture, because she ignores the impact which America imposes on the psyche of those who grow up in it. The necessities, the responsibilities, even, engendered by this impact are the issues in favor of which Dev returns to America. They are the issues by which Williams himself tests Eliot's and Pound's validity and finds them wanting. The curious coincidence of Dev's scientific training and his artistic interests makes him a peculiarly unconventional American. One feels that somehow the struggle with Europe is fairer than we sometimes find it in the uninstructed characters of other innocents abroad. In *A Voyage to Pagany* it is the critical best of America competing in superb style with the best of Europe, and while the outcome is not at all a cheap or easy victory for the home team, it is at least not a stalemate. The conflict has provided a fierce work-out from which the protagonist goes home refreshed and re-born in self-knowledge.

· · · ·

When Williams' first collection of short stories came out during the days of the Depression, it had a grimly appropriate title. *The Knife of the Times*, published in 1932, appears to represent the "real" world Dev Williams had gone back to at the end of *A Voyage to Pagany*. Pagany is no longer an operative ideal in these powerful, often humorously forthright stories of the bleak and sometimes heroic lives of the small people of America, many of whom are the cast-off spawn of that Europe which Dev could not accept.

The social types represented are diverse. Farm-boys, professional men, Negro servant-girls, middle-class housewives, local playboys, school teachers, the range of caste and personality is as wide as the landscape of a semiurban American community permits, although the locale shifts from industrial towns like Paterson, to near-by farm communities, and to unnamed suburban villages. The stories, although various in theme, seem to cluster about two poles: the present, represented by the title piece, "The

Knife of the Times," and the past, seen with a nostalgic authenticity of detail, and cherished for its greater fluidity of personality, its slower levelling-down of conduct and individuality. Sometimes, as in "An Old Time Raid" or "The Colored Girls of Passenack—Old and New," the present serves as ironic counterpoint to the freer, more careless style of American life in the early decades of the century.

Williams utilizes, perhaps not at all consciously, three sources for the predominant narrative style in this collection. Gertrude Stein's cadenced, clear, syntactically functional prose is suggested over and over again in the easy colloquial flow of the writing. The brilliantly swift title story is a small masterpiece (under six pages in length) of understatement, dealing with great delicacy of the curious, overpowering love of a middle-aged mother of six for her childhood friend, Maura, also the mother of a family. The lucid, almost transparently simple prose races along with Ethel's mounting lust, without any of the locutions of Miss Stein's later mannered writing, and more in the style of her early *Three Lives*.

At the time the stories in *A Knife of the Times* were being written, Williams was carefully studying Gertrude Stein's work, as a magazine piece [4] in which her emphasis on the "play" (or music) of sight, sense and sound contrasts were suggestively compared to that of Sterne's, especially as seen in Chapter 43 of *Tristram Shandy*. "Stein's theme," says Williams, "is writing." This had, of course, been his own theme in *The Great American Novel*. Further: "It is simply the skeleton, the 'formal' parts of writing, those

[4] See "The Work of Gertrude Stein" in *Pagany*, vol. 1, no. 1, Winter 1930, pp. 41–46.

that make form, that she has to do with, apart from the 'burden' which they carry." Williams does not deflesh the skeleton, as does Miss Stein in her later writing (this was not her practice in *Three Lives* and Williams in this article shows that he is aware of it), but instead makes the skeleton *compose* or bear the burden. A short passage from *A Knife of the Times* will show how much Williams has learned from the prose of Miss Stein's "Melanctha" (which he calls "one of the best bits of characterization produced in the United States") and how freely he employs it for narrative movement:

Ethel wrote letters now such as Maura wished she might at some time in her life have received from a man. She was told that all these years she had been dreamed of, passionately, without rival, without relief. Now, surely, Maura did not dare show the letters any longer to her husband. He would not understand.

The story moves with a compelling intensity to its surprising denouement in which the passive Maura is swept through sympathy into the vortex of her more aggressive friend's desire. The taut austerity of the style both heightens and contends with the desperately purposive passion of the distraught woman. The title of the story, suggesting as it does, another dimension of social reference for Maura's capitulation to Ethel, clarifies the ironic symbolism of lives, turned by the cruel edge of a mechanical society back upon themselves (upon their own narcissistic love-images) for enrichment and satisfaction.

In "The Sailor's Son," Williams handles the complementary situation to Lesbianism, in the behavior of the docile and dependent Manuel. The plot is clever, although not in the fashionable way. The revelation at the end does not depend on a trick of withheld knowledge for its shock, but derives from the actual opening up of the meaning of Manuel's conduct before the outraged eyes of his employer, Mrs. Cuthbertson. When Margie, the woman whom Manuel plans to marry and who supports him in periods of unemployment, is told by Mrs. Cuthbertson that she has fired Manual because of her discovery of his homosexuality, she completely reverses the direction of Mrs. Cuthbertson's judgment as well as the actual events of the story:

The boy is lonesome up here, said the woman. Why do you keep his friends away? I am engaged to marry him, I don't care what he does. Why should you worry? . . . Finally the fiancée grew abusive and Mrs. Cuthbertson losing her temper very nearly struck her. It was a wild moment. But in the end Manual was fired. And the woman took him back to the city with her where she told him she would pay for a room until she could find work for him elsewhere.

"The Descendant of Kings" is another story whose narrative cadences suggest a close reading of Stein. The process of Stewie's being and becoming are appropriately woven together in a supple, limpid prose. The handsome, summer playboy, Stewie, grows up in ignorance and want under the possessive guardianship of a poetic grandmother who keeps him out of school so that she can remain near her beloved sea. The story for its overtones of inarticulate, almost pathological deprivation stands alongside Sherwood Anderson's memorable portrait in "I'm A Fool" of another American possessed by his social inadequacies. When Stewie, still in his teens, gets out of the Navy up to which time "he had gone on like a straw on the stream of the old lady's will" he faces up to the fact that he knows nothing to do. Aimlessly, he falls for a sophisticated summer visitor, an artist's model, Muriel, who in her wisdom clarifies for him what is to be his role.

When he catches Muriel with another man (the inevitable Yale graduate), he gets the first of a series of singularly ironic blows which he is to get from women—always where it hurts him most. Later Stewie becomes a performer in the local hotel orchestra and his triumphs become almost epical. But the second time Stewie really falls, this time for a pretty schoolteacher, her double-crossing is fatal to his chief excellence. The understatedly symbolic denouement comes in Stewie's curious tussle with a bull in which, injured and bleeding, he finally conquers the animal by a heroic wrench of the nose-ring. It is the first time Stewie has ever tested his strength against another male. The struggle restores his psychic potentials for once again fulfilling his male nature. A revitalization or rebirth has taken place, and we know that Stewie will resume the career destined for him by his motherless, sea-haunted childhood. But the wry ending lowers the key of this victory over self, and we see that the protagonist is not immune from time any more than he is from the paradoxes of his own conquests: "For he did get over it fairly well in the end tho' he was never again as able as he had been as a kid—naturally."

Belle, the plump, middle-aged country Venus of "Pink and Blue" is a female Stewie in the fervor and single-mindedness of her pursuit of the opposite sex. But her touching addiction to the outer proprieties of caste, such as clothes, calling cards, and legal titles are seen at the level of a semicomic social criticism, different from the more inward conflict which determines Stewie's downward path to wisdom. For Belle is placidly at peace with herself in the amorous adventures which prove so destructive to the men who love her. Her confusions are merely social in their nature and it is the man who can give her the greatest quantity of matched "outfit" who, in the end, may keep her love. The story is told from the point of view of Mrs. Bandler, the employer of one of Belle's indeterminately numbered husbands. The tone of controlled irony derived from her gracious, kindly and equally caste-conscious viewpoint lends a quiet dignity to the pathetic events of this rural comedy.

"Mind and Body," as the title indicates, is similarly polarized around a conflict in values, a conflict which is finally resolved by the somewhat unsatisfactory deus-ex-machina of science, an engine the doctor employs when all other attempts to explain his psychotic patient to herself have failed. His reliance on the findings of capillaroscopy, "a study of the microscopic terminal blood vessels," is used self-consciously and with a deliberate obliquity of intention. The woman, a self-described manic-depressive with a background of institutionalization, is a fine study of the conflict between a primitive cultural inheritance and a veneer of the most esoteric sort of book-learning. Brilliant, educated, and miscast in her social and sexual role as wife to a kindly, lame, and womanish little male-nurse, she alternates between superstitious misapprehensions of her own physical condition and learned speculations on

213

literature and philosophy. The factor of suppressed Lesbianism in her personality which the doctor boorishly brings to the surface is appropriately left unresolved.

The sources of her problems in an inheritance from one of the "old country families" with its increment of insanity and pathology are only lightly sketched in. Nevertheless, by the time the rambling story, largely told by the patient herself, is completed we have a bold character drawing of a ruined human potential for social responsibility. These meanings do not lie close to the surface in "Mind and Body" any more than they do elsewhere in Williams' deceptively simple prose.

By now we can see that one of Williams' recurring aims in the short story is to achieve a reversal of values. "The Buffalos" because of its theme of the power-conflict between male and female, its rather explicit symbolism and the way in which the action is narrowed down to a male and female actor (thus intensifying the character of the conflict) reminds one of some of D. H. Lawrence's stories. A love affair between a beautiful suffragette and a man who is at first amused and then bored by her political ardors is brought to its frustrating, almost cruel, conclusion by the careful analogy with which the now disenchanted lover confronts the lady, for he has rightly suspected her motivation. The situation has been completely reversed: the suitor is the victor, but he has suffered a loss in the winning. Similarly, the lady has won her point: she has been theoretically granted the possession of the male privileges she envies. But having been taken at her word, she loses her man.

Two stories in *The Knife of the Times* reveal a special

214

attempt to come to grips with character as it responds to or stems from American social habit and values. When character is treated on a humorous, anecdotal level as in "An Old Time Raid," the story becomes essentially a study in manners. But in "Old Doc Rivers" the study of a brilliant, hopped-up suburban doctor, one of the richest character drawings of comparable length in recent American fiction, the problem of motivation is more deeply investigated. The social environment is reported, as in "An Old Time Raid," but it is also questioned. In "An Old Time Raid" the result is comedy, while in "Old Doc Rivers," although comic elements are present, the effect is one of tragedy.

In the first story "Dago" Schultz, the professional roisterer and good-time Charlie of a cocky, crude-mannered semiurban culture, expresses the gross animal vitality and instinctive insubordination of a raw, vital people. Dago's death (he was an expert train-hopper), while hopping a train after a drinking bout, is meaningless as "tragedy" but has a cultural significance. As the first-person narrator, commenting on his death, says: "Makes me think of an old man I knew, when they'd ask him how far back he could remember he'd say: I can remember back to when the U.S. was a republic.— That's where 'Dago' Schultz belongs. You know."

But if Dago is seen as a type of socially misdirected energy, still he is essentially part of his community, while Old Doc Rivers, the most able, talented and sensitive man in the New Jersey town where he practises, is shown as a man in conflict with his environment, his profession and his times. His drug-taking, which at first fortifies and then

increasingly hampers the execution of his brilliant diagnostic insights, is evaluated by the young colleague who
is narrator:

It came of his sensitivity, his civility; it was this that made him
do it, I'm sure; the antithesis rather of that hog-like complacency
that comes to so many men following the successful scamper for
cash.

The crude environment of the turn of the century times
"in the provincial bottom of the New Jersey" in which
Rivers lived, made it impossible for him to find a release
there, although at first he had great popularity and great
power.

Rivers' personality is built up through the younger
doctor's investigation of old hospital records for evidence
of Rivers' medical results, as well as through the various
eye-witness anecdotes which he collects from older patients and physicians. The social data are looked into with
the detachment of a field sociologist, but the cumulative
detail mounts to a profound study of individual character
while, curiously, forcing the social implications to a higher
level of abstraction. The

awful fever of overwork . . . A trembling in the arms and thighs,
a tightness of the neck and in the head above the eyes—fast breath,
vague pains in the muscles and in the feet. Followed by an orgasm,
crashing the job through, putting it over in a feverish heat. Then
the feeling of looseness afterward. Not pleasant. But there it is.
Then cigarettes, a shot of gin. And that's all there is to it. Women
the same, more and more . . . He had no time, had to be fast, he
had to improvise and did—to a marvel.

These are the social terms by which sensitive men like
Rivers must live. But as the tempo of the American malady

makes deeper inroads on Rivers' interior resources and capacity for rebound, he grows more dependent on drugs. Finally, he makes errors in judgment and eventually whispers of malpractice spring up. But still the humble butchers, the peasant mill-workers and street laborers go to him, for now his name has come to have mythic properties and the visible evidence of his professional defections are discounted. What the people of Creston want is what the unheeded voice of a collective Paterson cries out for in the poem *Paterson:* "A marvel, a marvel!" Even when he was almost "finished," the town's ritualistic faith in Rivers persists.

Rivers does not die in the gutter, as a conventional oracle might predict, but, what is worse, he is *through* before he quits. He is a man robbed of his full scope for action by the slow attrition of his personality through the very means by which it is completed. "Old Doc Rivers" is a self-contained, under-stated, and, perhaps, minor American tragedy. But in the compass of a forty-page story Williams has succeeded by a quiet, almost statistical investigation in piecing together the social meaning of the failure of a superb talent, "a serious indictment against all the evangelism of American life which I most hated."

. . . .

In his next volume of stories *Life Along the Passaic River* (1938) Williams confines himself almost entirely to the people who live along its banks. The collection, without being "regional," builds up a solid feeling of community, of place. Written during the Depression years, they reflect some of the curious dislocations in caste and character precipitated by the times. The Poles, the Italian mothers, the wild children, the unemployed, the furtive adolescents, all these aspects of the life of a small industrial town in America are explored with that warm authenticity of observation which sheds clarity and illumination into the disordered areas of the human soul. Many of the stories, like Chekhov's, have quite patently grown out of Williams' medical experience. Of these the best are "The Girl With the Pimply Face," "The Use of Force," "A Night in June," "Four Bottles of Beer," and "A Face of Stone." The last is one of Williams' finest stories, and demonstrates his secure movement in the limpid, Flaubertian prose which he was to consolidate so powerfully in *White Mule*.

In "A Face of Stone," a busy pediatrician is irritated by the seemingly deliberate obtuseness of a Jewish immigrant couple who come to him for the care of their child. The pattern follows that of Williams' most successful stories—a situation in which a reversal of values is achieved by the slow impact of character upon character. The story opens on a note of annoyance:

"He was one of these fresh Jewish types you want to kill at sight, the presuming poor whose looks change the minute cash is mentioned. But they're insistent, trying to force attention, taking advantage of good nature at the first crack. You come when I call you, that type. . . . She, on the other hand, looked Italian, a goaty slant to her eyes, a face often seen among Italian immigrants . . . A face of stone. It was an animal distrust, not shyness . . . She looked dirty. So did he . . ."

The patients do not follow the doctor's directions either in the care of their child or in calling upon his services.

The overtones of the doctor's distaste for these uncoopera-
tive and unattractive people is expressed in terms of "racial
prejudice." Yet, in a gradual way, he begins to be involved in their problems. First it is the baby, with "a
perfectly happy fresh mug on him" that amuses him in
spite of himself. Then he becomes interested in the curious
dull flush which comes over the greasy little husband
whenever the inarticulate wife's health is discussed. Eventually, he learns that she is only twenty-four, that all her
relatives were killed in Poland, and that she had almost
no food as a child. The bare, medical description of the
woman's physical features builds up the pathos of her deprived past, but yet supports the doctor's wish to hold on
to his negative attitudes.

When he learns that the woman herself has recently
arrived from Poland he slowly begins to understand her
absorption in the baby. As the husband, on the last call,
describes how he must dissolve aspirin for her "His face
reddened again and suddenly I understood his half shameful love for the woman and at the same time the extent
of her reliance on him. I was touched." The doctor's own
growth in understanding seems to invade the woman with
the face of stone. When he shows her some pills for her
rheumatic pains, "She looked at them again. Then for the
first time since I had known her a broad smile spread all
over her face. Yeah, she said, I swallow him." That is the
end of the story. There is no explicit referral to the nature
of the exchange. But what has happened, in this restrained
narrative, its detail grounded in the natural orbit of the
doctor's job, is that a social miracle of a sort has been accomplished. Two opposed sets of impulse, training, and

value as represented by the worn, small-town American physician (working in a milieu remarkably like Williams' own Rutherford), and the obdurate, immigrant couple are brought into conflict. The outcome is that each begins to accept something from the other's realm of meaning. The harsh undertones of prejudice on the one hand and mistrust on the other are ruled out of the story by the expansive warmth of the final sentence.

In "The Girl With the Pimply Face" there is a similar struggle between two sets of values. The doctor-narrator, who in reality is the hero of the piece, takes a warm and understanding interest in a Russian working-class family. While visiting their sick baby, the doctor gets interested in a pimply-faced girl of sixteen, the sister, who by her tough, straightforward self-reliance amuses him. He learns that she has left school and advises her on how to care for her face. Later, he meets the family's former physician who tells him they are drunks, on the charity rolls, that they mistreat the baby and that the girl is a "little bitch. Say, if I had my way I'd run her out of town tomorrow morning . . . Boy, they sure took you in." But when the doctor returns he finds the baby improved, the girl's face clearing up and the girl going back to school. There is no attempt to whitewash the people. The doctor, as opposed to his cynical colleague, may have been "taken in." He doesn't know, nor do we. But he has been fulfilling his function as healer. He has cured, and his fulfillment is in his willingness to accept the reward proper to his function, a reward which lies entirely in the curing. It is this type of subtle revaluation of a crass popular morality, which reveals Williams as a writer with the greatest responsiveness to the questions of social ethics.

In "The Use of Force," a very short story, the doctor-narrator emerges as the villain of the piece. The way in which the physician, in spite of his recognition that he is contending with a sick child, is gradually drawn into a violent contest of wills is depicted with honesty and power. The brutality with which the doctor, now in a blind rage, forces open the child's mouth and discovers the nature of the illness is a startling exposure of those subrational wells of impulse which invade the conduct of supposedly disciplined adults.

On the other side of the psychological scale, in "Jean Biecke," is the curiously unexpected love and tenderness which a very ill infant, dying of a seemingly undiagnosable ailment, arouses in the breasts of the hard-boiled doctor-narrator and the attending physicians and nurses. The miracle of human personality is the beautiful center of the relationship. Williams is one of the few writers of fiction who are aware of the dynamics of this force in infants:

Somehow or other, I hated to see that kid go. Everybody felt rotten. She was such a scrawny, misshapen, worthless piece of humanity that I had said many times that somebody ought to chuck her in the garbage chute—but after a month watching her suck up her milk and thrive on it—and to see those alert blue eyes in that face—well, it wasn't pleasant.

The tiny thread by which the potentials of personality develop or are cut off is revealed, at the end, to have been a slip-up in diagnostic procedure for which several interested and capable physicians are jointly responsible.

"A Night in June" is a warmly stated tale of a physician's home delivery of a child to a simple Italian woman who can hardly talk with him. There is profound humility in the doctor's awareness of how his own responses to the woman have changed: "This woman in her present condition would have seemed repulsive to me ten years ago—now, poor soul, I saw her to be as clean as a cow that calves. The flesh of my arm lay against the flesh of her knee gratefully. It was I who was being comforted and soothed." Her child is born, the doctor and the mother jointly assisting the delivery. In the end, the doctor has been strengthened and renewed by his closeness to the woman's experience.

"At the Front," like "Four Bottles of Beer," relies on first-person narrative for a brief and humorously anecdotal tale of World War I. Both this and the series of small vignettes collected in the end-piece, "World's End," seem to have been set down because of Williams' persistent interest in speech patterns as ends in themselves, as well as hallmarks of personality. Several sketches in "World's End" deal with the meaningless but nevertheless deadly violence with which the human and the animal worlds combat one another. The one of the old hospital infested with cats which the internes hunt down and destroy for twenty-five cent bonuses, or that of the laboratory where the clotted blood on slides is eaten overnight by invading cockroaches are curiously moving glimpses of man's vulnerability to physical degradation. These tales grow out of experiences Williams had over thirty years before when interning in the ramshackly, ill-administered

Nursery and Child's Hospital in a New York slum district.

In "Dance Pseudo Macabre" in which the reader follows a doctor on his emergency rounds in the middle of the night, Williams defends the use of this kind of material. He defies those who would accuse him of a "shallow" morbidity to prove that health alone is inevitable: "I defend the normality of every distortion to which the flesh is susceptible, every disease, every amputation." Although "Dance Pseudo Macabre" is not one of William's successful pieces, others of these tales of death and illness compel us to accept his valuation. These stories do not depress us but instead instruct us in a greater comprehension of the narrow boundaries between living and dying, between health and disease, between reason and impulse. For Williams' sane, compassionate and scientific intellect orders these complex relationships from the uniquely privileged vantage point of one whose profession is equally among the quick and the dead. These stories will prove revealing sources for Williams' future biographers.

The most ambitious story of *Life Along the Passaic* is "The Dawn of Another Day." The time is the Depression and a young man of background and wealth has, in desperation, left his wife and children who are now living off his mother-in-law, to stay on an old unsaleable yacht. His companion is a chronic drunk, Fred, who drinks his liquor and stimulates him by his undisciplined talk of revolution, and the defections of the class to which Ed, the younger man, belongs. The servants are loyal to Ed's family, even supplying them with food, and Ed himself has his laundry cared for by a young colored woman, Pauline.

On the particular dark evening of the story, the two odd friends are drinking and arguing about Communism on Ed's boat. Finally, Fred falls into a drunken sleep and Ed, going ashore, meets Pauline who has called for his wash. He is grateful and offers to walk her down the road. He is troubled and lonely and begins to talk to her. She, however, is responding on another level and suggests as much. Ed is startled but, nevertheless, attracted by her offer, although earlier in the evening he had warned Fred to stay away from the Negro women living along the river-bank unless he wished to risk a venereal disease. Now Pauline, with a curious dignity, withdraws until she is sure she is really wanted.

The two go back to the yacht where Fred lies in a drunken stupor and the colored woman (who perhaps has had an encounter with Fred) keeps urging that Ed "throw the bum out." Pauline's sexual vitality restores Ed's sense of belief in himself. He tries to communicate to her that it has shaken up his scale of values. " 'Do you know where I feel it most?' Ed went on slowly. 'In the head.' She chuckled and moved against him." The "class-consciousness" in which Fred has tried to instruct him is illuminated by his random but meaningful experience with Pauline. As they walk along on her way to her home she again tells Ed to "kick that dirty bum out . . . He isn't in your class." Ed's attitude toward Pauline is grateful but clean-cut: ". . . I'm not getting rid of that guy. That's final . . ." It is clear, too, that he is not going to turn to his family for release from the hard way he has chosen. A victory is implied for Ed, although we do not know precisely what kind. We sense that he has chosen what is, in effect, a novitiate toward a better understanding of life.

The irony of the revelation that Ed has experienced lies, of course, in the fact that its instrument, Pauline, has no consciousness of it. But Ed sees, and this is the point at which the story is relieved from a possible charge of romanticism, that it was the disorganized Fred who led him in the direction of the revolt which Pauline merely symbolically fulfilled.

The weakness of this story is not in its tone which is subtly and beautifully modulated to catch the undercurrents of insecurity and tension between the colored woman and the white man, between the professional has-not and the amateur has-been, but in an inadequate development of the connection between Ed's physical knowledge of Pauline and his implied acceptance of Fred's analysis of society.

．　．　．　．

When Williams wrote his ambitious comedy of American manners *White Mule*, begun as far back as 1927,[5] the "class-consciousness" of the characters was not planned as part of their own consciousness. But the struggle for caste differentiation has now become one of the important themes. Although *White Mule* seems, from the start, to have been conceived as a trilogy, the title of the first

[5] See *The Writer*, August 1937, " 'White Mule' Versus Poetry," in which Williams describes the genesis and history of *White Mule*. Begun in 1927 "The first chapters lay about the attic for several years . . . I at first intended to interweave a contrasting story of other people with this but in the end under the advice of Richard Johns, publisher of *Pagany*, I decided not to do so." Many of the chapters in *White Mule* were published in *Pagany* and *The Magazine*.

225

volume apparently was projected as the title of the whole. *White Mule,* published in 1937, was followed by the second book, *In the Money,* in 1940, and the two were subsequently reprinted in 1946 in one volume and re-titled, somewhat confusingly, *First Act. The Build-Up,* planned as the third volume of the trilogy, is now in progress.[6]

White Mule deals with the spiritual and social growth of the Stecher family in the early years of the century as they seek to assimilate themselves to the dominant mores and values of the new world they have chosen for their field of action. The plan of the trilogy has been succinctly outlined by Williams in *The Writer:*

In this volume (*White Mule*) the baby has her "pattern" set. In the next volume she learns how to dress herself at about the age of three. In the last volume she gets as far as the first things she will later remember . . . While she is doing this, the family makes money and moves into the country. The third volume will end without the baby as a principal character. It has to. The social theories of yesterday finally become arthritic and Joe (the father) dies among their rigidities . . .

Book III, will be the "build-up" of the family for the sake of the suburban town where, in their new affluence, they take root. Gurlie Stecher begins to put on front, to plan a strategy for the social implementation of the family into the community's élite. But, because of Joe Stecher's origins, the family is caught in the hatreds of World War I and their social collapse occurs when the town turns on them even while the United States is neutral. Williams sees this not as tragedy but as social comedy, although he is

[6] One chapter was published in *Briarcliff Quarterly,* Williams Issue, October 1946.

prepared to let the book determine its tone—to some extent—in the writing.[7]

Williams' first interest in writing the novel is clearly stated in *The Writer:*

The writing of the language is what interests me. So in writing *White Mule* my greatest concern was to write with attention to marshalling the words into an order which would be free from "lies." . . .

Oh, yes, there is a story. I'm a pediatrician, I take care of babies and try to make them grow. I enjoy it. Nothing is more appropriate to a man than an interest in babies. He should today substitute his interest for that of the obsolete mother. Women today merely have babies. It takes a man to bring them up. And it had better be a man with an interest in a good style in order that we don't load up the little composition with "lies." It's not easy.

However, if a particular background must be located for his approach to the novel, Williams feels it is Flaubertian. His wish is to reveal what he sees without comment, to record not what he *should* observe, but what he does observe. He is especially anxious to eliminate the "I," to write as if from another world. This genuine desire to annihilate the "self" in art has come to Williams as a process of slow growth. It was otherwise, as we have seen, in *The Great American Novel* where the writing was grounded in an axiomatic first cause: "I begin with myself."

In *White Mule* Williams begins with society. The wish to "annihilate" the self may be seen as merely an inverted mysticism, or an ascetic discipline of self-deception but that seems an over-sophistical view of the artist's motiva-

[7] The description of the projected third volume of *White Mule* is based on a conversation with Dr. Williams in June or July, 1946.

tion for the role in which he casts the self. The "self" in creation is, of course, a *sina qua non*. But to know whether we get to it through the texture of the social world which the artist compels for our attention, or whether we get it as it filters through itself the data of the "real" world is useful. These distinctions make better sense than labels like objective or subjective as descriptions of the novelist's approach to his materials.

The first chapter of *White Mule*, "To Be," shows how the scientist, in the radical sense of the word, disciplines the artist on a subject where romantic notions often take over the real work of observation. "To Be," emphasizing the potentials of the child who is to be the central character of the novel, is the best description of childbirth that I know of in fiction. The writing of "To Be" considerably antedates the rest of the novel, closely following *A Voyage to Pagany*, and this explains a certain similarity in style. Nevertheless, although it was not until ten years later that the novel was completed, the direction of *White Mule* is implicit in the first chapter; or, to put it another way, *White Mule* fulfills the potentials of "To Be."

If Williams had written no other piece of fiction, "To Be" would mark him as a significant worker in that medium. It begins:

She entered, as Venus from the sea, dripping. The air enclosed her, she felt it all over her touching, waking her. If Venus did not cry aloud after release from the pressures of that sea-womb, feeling the new and lighter fluid springing in her chest, flinging out her arms—this one did. Screwing up her tiny smeared face, she let out three convulsive yells—and lay still.

Stop that crying, said Mrs. D, you should be glad to get outa that hole.

It's a girl. What? A girl. But I wanted a boy. Look again. It's a girl, Mam. No! Take it away. I don't want it. All this trouble for another girl.

What is it? said Joe, at the door. A little girl. That's too bad. Is it all right? Yes, a bit small though. . . .

In spite of the allusion to Venus, Williams' unwillingness to romanticize childbirth is visible at once. A modern romantic, for example, might have begun with the intra-uterine life of the child. Williams begins, quite sensibly, with what he knows and what is verifiable—the fact of birth. A physician is a kind of machinist to the body, and Williams, like other technicians, possesses an admiration for the super-machine that is even more complex than his skill.

This chapter announces some major themes of the trilogy. The basic theme is coming into the new or, *discovery*, which, as I have pointed out, is a perennial one in Williams' prose, poetry and aesthetics. Practically speaking, what could be newer than a baby fresh out of its mother's womb? The development of the first two novels is fundamentally in the narration of the baby's continued discovery of the new world she is in. By the time Flossie is about three, as Williams' own description of his plan indicates, the world is not so new, the bases of her personality structure are laid, and she no longer is the principal character. The Family, as a unit, takes over.

A secondary theme of some importance is stated in the third paragraph of "To Be." "Take it away," says Gurlie Stecher, "I don't want it." While never formulated as a generalization, a major fact in the baby's development is Gurlie's original rejection of her, followed by the puny child's refusal to take her mother's milk, and her subsequent struggle for recognition and acceptance in the family. Joe's dependence on Gurlie to furnish the emotional lead also works against the baby and this too is revealed in the opening sentences. Still, he is at least concerned for Flossie's well-being so that there is a loophole left through which the child may and, in fact, does creep into his affections.

Mrs. D., the shrewd, kindly, dirty-nailed midwife furnishes a cynical counterpoint which plays against the newness, the pristine, shining and altogether miraculous this-or-that-wayness which represents the potentialities of the baby. The midwife is in the worldly, tolerant, "anti-poetic" tradition of the Nurse in *Romeo and Juliet* or of the good wife of Bath. She harangues the baby from the point of view of a somewhat superstitious "experience":

About five pounds is my guess. You poor little mite, to come into a world like this one. Roll over here and stop wriggling or you'll be on the floor. Open your legs now till I rub some of this oil in there. You'll open them glad enough one of these days—if you're not sorry for it. So in all of these creases. How it sticks. It's like lard. I wonder what they have that in them for. It's hard to be born a girl . . . She parted the little parts looking and wondering at their smallness and perfection and shaking her head forebodingly.

The entire chapter, as it develops the struggle between the mother and the willful ugly child, is magnificently written. The baby's rebelliousness, its voice of a "penetrating puniness" begins to dominate the environment.

The rich synthesis of fact and tone in "To Be" is a slightly heightened prelude to the more unilinear, chronological development of the other chapters. Soon lines of the family conflict are more sharply drawn. Joe, an expert printer, is shown in all the confusions of his thwarted love of fine craftsmanship as he finds the money emphasis of America hateful but, nevertheless, infectious. Gurlie's more aggressive Viking heritage, however, manifests itself in a love for conquest on the conqueror's own terms. She uses the fact that they now have two daughters to prod Joe's gentler ambitions. It is not just work that will get him money, she insists, but brains which he has and is afraid to use.

. . . I am going to live and see the world and I must have money. And you are going to make it for me.

Don't talk about things you don't understand, he replied. It's you that don't understand. You think you know everything you Dutchies. You have got to study people, like me.

What for, he said, to skin them?

No, to make use of them.

Joe's simple analysis of labor problems, stems not only from Gurlie's money orientation but from his own background. "In Berlin men worked. Here they had strikes to get more money . . . That's not the way. Everybody should work the best that he knows how . . . Men should work and they should be paid." In his confusion and failure to understand the nature of the American dream, Joe looks for a place to lay responsibility.

It's the Irish, he thought to himself, and the Sheenies. Those are the suckers who spoil everything. They don't like good work. Money, that's all, money. . . . America . . . rose in his clear mind as something beyond the grasp of reason, something mediaeval, ignorant, arrogant—at once rich and cheap. A battle for something without value at the cost of all that he knew of that was worthwhile.

231

What Joe knows is "a material honesty, a logic of work and pay."

But as the baby begins to thrive after the first grim months, Gurlie's pressure on Joe becomes more insistent. As responsibilities begin to press upon him, Joe tends to fix more and more upon the unions as the enemy. His own economic role as a kind of straw boss (it is he who does the planning and estimating for the printing firm which employs him) shows him that the workingmen are against him and that it will be necessary to take a stand. Joe's decision comes at a little party to celebrate the arrival of his brother Oscar who is in the meat-packing business in Chicago. The Stechers and their guests drink up and presently all the family tensions come to the surface. Oscar, an indulgent, pleasure-loving man is a member of the meat-packers' union and this knowledge, together with Gurlie's half-drunken taunts, impels Joe to give a toast, "Down with the unions," in which the others do not join.

In summarizing, I tend to generalize about motivation, although such generalizations do not occur in *White Mule*. For example, it becomes apparent that the crystallization of Joe's divided feeling on unions is motivated by a suppressed jealousy of Oscar's freedom (the latter is a bachelor who had earlier run off with another man's wife), and his resentment that as a child he had taken on the family's burdens as bread-winner, while, even yet, Oscar can change jobs with the casualness of a man changing neckties. But none of these facts are presented serially to "explain" Joe's behavior. There is merely the simple account of the party and the seemingly casual talk out of which we ourselves must make the appropriate analytical de-

232

ductions. Williams' method in the trilogy is to get at the structure of experience by giving us its texture. Sometimes, in fact, *White Mule* seems all texture. In "Conflict," the chapter I am discussing, the narrative appears merely to develop the family relationships, to further depict a homey, half-European middle-class heartiness, but in reality it advances our understanding of the social and historical dynamics which animate these very qualities. It can be said of Williams that in his recent fiction it is texture which exposes structure. That is, his structure, the skeleton which as omniscient narrator he suppresses, can only be known and exposed through texture.[8]

To return to the "story": When Joe's shop goes on strike, Joe sides with his employers. Still, there is evidence that his conscience bothers him, for he surreptitiously visits the home of one of the "troublemakers," a drunken Irish printer, Carmody, whose pitiful wife has asked for reconsideration for her husband. The evident dignity of the woman's care for her five children in their foul quarters moves Joe to offer to advance a week's salary if Carmody shows up sober for work. Carmody returns drunk and with a drunk's uncanny intuition senses there has been a visitor. There is a brutal fight in which the man "a prince-of-the-barroom-type" but "lean and built for courage" beats his wife unmercifully while the cowering children look on in terror. The economically stated fight, together with the depiction of the children, makes this one of the

---

[8] It will be recognized that I am borrowing John Crowe Ransom's suggestive use of the terms "structure" and "texture" in his discussions of poetry. This should not suggest, however, that Williams writes "poetic" prose.

most powerful chapters in *White Mule*. It is one which says more than could several tracts about the confused motives, the sharp impingements of necessity upon original nature, which create the mysterious differentials of "personality," even in a seemingly deterministic poverty.

Underneath the deceptively simple surface of Williams' prose, a prose which might be considered "behavioristic" in the sense that we are told what people do and say and think but not what they *are* or *why* they do and think as they do, is a deep belief in the vast variety and uniqueness of human personality. It is this belief which motivates his interest in Flossie. The baby is "mysterious" because while we see all the things she does, and that are done to her, it is Flossie's own potentials for responding to her environment which are the determinants of the "person" she is to be. The mid-wife, Mrs. D., in one of the early pages, observes: "That baby's got a temper . . . In about two days you begin to notice a difference in them. They're no two of them alike." Williams, for all his interest in the social surfaces of living, is, at bottom, a kind of Aristotelian realist rather than a Watsonian behaviorist, or an economic determinist. It is the unorthodoxy of this point of view in fiction which makes Williams' prose seem flat and featureless to those who are used to the visibly dramatic orbits of cause and effect around which most novels rotate.

Revealingly, a wry, over-excited little pediatrician to whom Gurlie takes the puny Flossie presents Williams' view of "education" as it develops personality. The famous doctor is a thinly disguised Williams:

What's the matter with the child? It makes me laugh. The child's alive, that's what's the matter with the child. . . . What's the matter with the children? They are unhappy . . . Almost, one should say, they're born to be unhappy. Every generation kills the next's chances of being happy in its children—out of envy. Malice, I tell you . . . We build schools. Schools, mind you, those factories of despair. Fools, that's what it rhymes with.

Although the doctor can't put his finger on anything specifically wrong with Flossie, his advice is to take her to the country. "A summer in New York will kill her."

Up in Vermont, on a farm with an old Swedish couple, Gurlie's powerful personality comes to the fore. But the old, hard-working Paysons to whom she tries to express her feelings about America are not convinced of Vermont's perfections. For the summer, yes. Or "With only a little money, I could be happy here," says Mr. Payson. And as Gurlie tries to define why she came to America, she becomes thoughtful. She came to America only because of money but now she wonders if Europe would be "too slow" for her. "Everything is set. Everyone stays in his own class." But she is proud of her ancestors, of her "strong, healthy people." She is sufficiently the healthy, insensitive animal herself to wish "If all the people in the world were like us, what a fine place it would be."

The ironic counterpoint to Gurlie's idyllic but somehow sinister contentment follows upon the heels of this scene, in Chapter XX, "The Soundout." It is here that Joe Stecher makes the final capitulation to the American "big business" values which will continue to make Gurlie's peace of mind possible. Mr. Lemon, who is to be the silent partner in Joe's projected firm sounds him out on his labor history and his business ethics. He is disturbed when Joe indicates that he doesn't like the stock market, saying "It is a swindle." Mr. Lemon tells him that he is identifying a man's private character with business and that Joe will not be able to do business that way. Mr. Lemon warns Joe that they are going to have a fight on their hands, and "It'll be a dirty fight too."

Subconsciously, Joe knows there are ambiguities in the line of action he has chosen. These ambiguities are subtly developed as he watches a ball game next day while his mind recapitulates the terms of his new enterprise. He tries to rationalize his feeling of guilt toward his employers (for he continues working for them while setting up his rival business), on the grounds that they never gave a fair bid in their lives. As the game ends and he wanders toward the pitcher's mound, Joe notices how much it is raised above the rest of the diamond: "That's just it, he said, when you really get close to a thing." The soft grass beyond "was coarser than he thought it to be from the stands, much more uneven and full of worm casts."

Joe's increasing premonition of his eventual involvement with the corrupt forces he will of necessity compete with is nowhere generalized, for Williams, as I have remarked, is trying to omit the commenting "I" and Joe himself is unable to generalize his situation. But the raised mound and the pock-marked field provide details which allow us to do the evaluation concretely. Although Joe may not, we do see the analogy between his view from the stand and close up with that of his business venture, seen in blueprint, or in the field of action. We have assisted the process of the novel in allowing texture to reveal connections, joinings, structure. So, the once-famous but now decrepit baseball player with whom Joe has chatted at the game, in the specific context of Joe's anxieties, becomes a ghostly warning of the hollow rewards of "success." It is the reader who must make this connection, which the author, "writing from another world," has suppressed.

. . . .

The legend on the flyleaf of *In the Money* published in 1940, states it is "a sequel to *White Mule*. The political pitch of this novel is several years later than the first; the theme continues as before." The opening dialogue between the Vermont storekeeper and Gurlie now clarifies the title, *White Mule*. It is the storekeeper's inspiration to connect little Flossie's stubbornness with her white face, and he calls her a little White Mule after a particularly potent local whiskey. It is typical of Williams' indirection to leave this explanation for the sequel, just as it was in keeping with his disinterest in merely physical characteristics which withheld a description of Joe's appearance until the end of *White Mule*.

Technically, *In the Money* relies on the same approach as *White Mule* with the exception of the quotation marks to designate speech used in the former. The author's note on the jacket of *First Act* (the joint reissue of both novels in 1946) asks that the reader decide whether ". . . *In the Money* is a better book by virtue of the quotation marks, or otherwise?" There is no question where Williams' own choice would lie. As he breezily puts it:

Who cares who's saying what? The thing is to tune in on the thing that's happening. Tune in, pick it up fast, put it together to make sense, to know what's going on. Isn't that it? What are people? Who

237

cares whether or not it's a man or a woman talking. Oh, character! We're all the characters . . . Why bother who says it so long as it gets said? . . . Any individual is twenty persons of all ages and sexes, any one of which might say anything.

While Williams' plea is theoretically persuasive, the fact of the matter is that there is no ambiguity in *White Mule* as to the identity of the speaker, even without the quotation marks. This is precisely what one should expect from a writer as attentive to speech mannerisms as is Williams.

At the conclusion of *In the Money* the Stechers are "in." But the price of this arrival is costly for Joe; and the family, especially little Flossie, reflects his inner strain. Gurlie's development may be taken as symptomatic of the novel's movement as a whole. For Gurlie, healthy, coarse, aware of her own animal magnetism, yet predominantly social rather than sensuous in her objectives, moves from a somewhat confused, though aggressive pestering of her "little Dutchie" to make more money, on to an imperious campaign to satisfy ego-needs which she summarizes by describing herself as "a sport."

At the end, Gurlie is clearly seen as the dominating axis of will and desire around which the Stecher household revolves. Williams does this by a slow, cumulative revelation of her egotism. Without analytic comment of any sort, there are the repeated incidents of Gurlie's limited responses to people who are not "big" or "on top." This comes out in her overbearing anti-semitism (her encounter with the Jewish mother and child in the park), her prudish lower middle-class Grundyism (her fury at the two unseen lovers occupying the neighboring stateroom on the Albany night-boat), her crudeness of bearing toward her own mother whom she actually orders out of her home, her bickering, insulting jealousy of Joe (when one of his female employees innocently comes to the home to ask for a job) through to the final pages of *In the Money* when Gurlie accuses her husband of discussing her with her own family, and hints at even greater disloyalties.

It is then too that we see the finality with which Gurlie has rejected Flossie, in all the aspects of the maternal role. And Joe is recognizably unhappy under Gurlie's now compulsive browbeating. Olga, Gurlie's sweet spinster sister, diagnoses the malady:

> "You never have enough," she said. "Like a child. Because you don't have as much as somebody else you want more and more. You even talk like a child . . . You make yourself unhappy. Look at Joe."

But Gurlie denies that she is unhappy, and in the next breath asks why she should be satisfied, adding with a laugh which is ominous for the family's future peace, "Wait and see."

Just as the tensions between Joe and Gurlie have become more sharply defined, so the whole of *In the Money* moves toward a clearer definition of the conflicts inherent in the texture of daily living in the United States. The inevitability with which the sociological "structure" of the novel is revealed through the texture of minutely particularized lives bears testimony to the high morality in which Williams', like Flaubert's "naturalism" is grounded. For the woman-motivated, woman-dominated society of modern America radiates out from Gurlie, a special and highly individualized product of Europe, to the shadowy Mrs. Lemon, the wife of Joe's backer, who moves on a loftier economic plane, and points to a critical flaw in the whole social fabric. Similarly, although the word "prejudice" does not occur, there is an accretion of incident, never pulled together by Williams into a generalization, which shows how the social mechanism of prejudice operates. When Joe is setting up his own business and old Wynnewood, his boss, learns of it there is much invective against Dutchmen and Heinies; when the family sees European immigrants at the pier, there is an amused and contemptuous curiosity on Gurlie's part which acknowledges no kinship with these people new to a country to which she herself does not yet belong. They are outsiders, like the Jews. Even little Elsa, the Finnish maid wants so desperately to "belong" that she resents the good speech of the Negro maids in the park who speak the language with manifest superiority over her own faltering attempts. There is also the Stechers' aloofness from community activities because Gurlie is feeling her way toward a milieu which will provide a greater challenge to her rapidly expanding ego.

And, as sociologists and psychologists tell us, it is the American male who pays by diminished stature for the ambivalent ego-drives of the female who cannot be satisfied with her traditional maternal role. Gurlie, of course, does not have the conflicts of the modern career-woman. Nevertheless, she is not adjusted to the mother-housewife role. Rejecting her impoverished Norwegian background and its rigid caste system, she is, nevertheless, both critical of and hostile to certain aspects of American living. She is instinctively, femalely possessive, acquisitive; thus emotionally and politically anti-democratic. She senses the dominant social symbol of her times to be the dollar bill, and it is in terms of this universally accepted emblem that she seeks to realize herself.

Joe, on the other hand, questions even while responding to this willful direction. While Gurlie is both inside and outside her American scheme of value, Joe, one feels, is always to remain the outsider. So detached is he, in reality, that at one point in the novel, after the battle for the government contract has been won by his unflagging exposure of chicanery, his backer, Mr. Lemon, says:

"You know, my suspicion is that in spite of all the magnificent fight you put up—in spite of all—I had the feeling and I still have it that you don't give a damn about the whole thing, from start to finish, nothing of it."

"Well," said Joe slowly, "that's putting it pretty strong. But I could have done something else, I suppose, and been much happier. Maybe."

. . .

"The only time I feel happy," said Joe, "is when I'm working."

By the end of *In the Money* the gulf between husband and wife is widening and Joe is looking for closer emotional attachments in his little daughters. The prestige-drives of Gurlie, we can be pretty certain, will never infect Joe (we have, for example, seen him turn down Lemon's offer to make him a member of his club) but, on the other hand, as we leave the family in their new suburban home, we know that he is irretrievably caught up in the self-perpetuating mechanism of "success" and that, more than the others, he is to be the sacrificial victim on the altar of their social "happiness."

The details of this societal analysis are magnificently

handled: one thinks of the crisp presentation of Joe's interview with Teddy Roosevelt where, unimpressed by the great man, the militant, self-possessed German immigrant sees through to the shallowness of the President's "policy" talk. Joe can fight effectively for the economic rewards offered by his society because, at bottom, he is really free of its values:

. . . You have to be an actor. You have to get all excited and make them think you want something desperately. You *have* to. They have to see it in your face, that you want money . . . You have to respect money. You owe it to them. You owe it to them because you're sorry for them, you have to show them that they're right.

But Joe knows that he pays a price, the businessman's price, for victory:

If he, Joe Stecher, hadn't played his game so as to put the pressure on when its effect would be most telling—what chance would he have had? Self-interest is a great benefactor, thought Joe.

All victory exacts a price and Joe happens to be clearer than most about the nature of his own. Joe's resourcefulness has laid wide open a scandal in which the public has been defrauded of its money. He has merely been a good businessman by keeping his own bid secret from firms whose own bids he was in a position to surmise. Still, one senses Joe's disenchantment with the quality of his triumph. For while his original gentleness has emerged from the fires of domestic conflict as a steelier substance, he retains an inner humility capable of distrusting it. His crusading exposure of graft in the Post Office Department after all lines his own pockets in the end. His motives have not been dishonest but in the complex game of outsmarting his rivals he must use some of their weapons. That is the paradox of the honest businessman who would be a "success." And Joe's difference from the business-man-hero of Dreiserian cut is that he is never once be-mused by reading a romantic parable into the catch-as-catch-can code of ethics of the world in which he must function.

Although I have stressed the sharpness with which the social tensions emerge in *In the Money*, this is but one of the structural elements in the novel. The psychological development of the children, particularly that of Flossie, is an equally important strand in the fabric of the Stechers' lives. Conflict between Gurlie and her mother precipitates a traumatic experience for Flossie which is to mark her for the rest of her life. The harsh voices of the fighting women have frightened the baby and when she is put to bed that evening, the rustling of a window shade, the uninterpretable night, all add to her terror. After Flossie is quieted, the night—who is the unseen antagonist—is made to say, "You'll see. You did it. I touched her. There will always be night a little written upon her brain." While this chapter is finely conceived and the child's inarticu-late anguish movingly portrayed, the departure from the scrupulous objectivity of the narrative is too radical. The personification of night, as well as the conventionality of her symbolic role, seems literary, a fault rare in Williams' work.

But Gurlie's final words restore the stylistic dynamics of the novel to their customary channels. As she is falling off to sleep she says: "It was the devil in her . . . I'll be glad to get rid of her." We are uncertain whether it is her mother, who is leaving the next day, or her daughter of whom Gurlie is speaking. But she emerges now as the unconsciously cruel and selfish agent of the unhappiness which both must face. More profoundly, this crucial chapter, repeating the conflict between the two generations (it had been Gurlie against her mother, now it is Gurlie against her daughter), dramatizes the unending chain of causality in the determination of the individual soul.

But to isolate these events is to suggest that they are the critical areas of meaning, whereas they are embedded in the richly varied although unmomentous texture of daily living. The children grow, meet other children in the park, make social explorations, get vaccinated, but all this is detailed as part of the flow of growth, quietly, with freshness of language and immediacy of observation. The simplicity with which these small doings are rendered, the implicitness with which "mood" is always embodied in event is illustrated in this passage:

"Come Lottie we'd better be going now," said Gurlie to her older daughter. She lay back for a moment on the soft grass with her hands under her head and looked up at the sun. The baby leaned over her and rested her head sidewise on her mother's breast. Lottie too came beside her mother and stood looking down at her.

This, of course, is a painter's composition but, as in a good picture, we accept the reality of the persons precisely because they are *composed;* it is the *grouping* which itself evokes the tenderness and the mystery of a special human relationship.

But it is Dr. Mabott, another slightly disguised Williams (how he enjoys these charming eccentric doctors!) who formulates the principles upon which the development of the children in the novel are based in his article "The Child's Development During the Second Year":

This is to be not a plant nor a mere animal but a human being. It begins to experience now its first independence—and the accidents which ensue. A larval year, largely hidden from our view—

. . . it gives the mind its enduring form. The universe expands now so rapidly for the small traveller, marooned as he is here, that a man may seek and will usually find all his excuses in misfortune for the rest of his days in what has taken place during this year . . .

The small prisoner has to be forced into the accidental mould of the life his or her parents find forced upon them in turn by their own more or less accidental economic and hereditary circumstances . . .

Williams rescues this "larval year . . . Buried and gone forever" and holds it, scientifically, curiously, and with a poet's sense of wonder up to the brilliant light of affectionate observation. The seemingly casual ebb and flow of little Flossie's life is one of the most original contributions to the imaginative literature of childhood in the English language. But Williams "places" the child as "father to the man," not in a mystic vacuum of clouds and glory, but in the real impinging social universe of people, objects and events with which it must come to terms through its unique adaptabilities, whether in poverty or "in the money." This is not an economic nor a behaviorist, any more than it is a Freudian, determinism. For it is the indomitable, fighting, something which is "Flossie" which will do the ordering of its accidents of experience. That is the final weight it seems to me, of Williams' Flaubertian "naturalism." It is, like Flaubert's, a critical naturalism and not a romantic one. "Perfectability" is only one of the infinite varieties of roads open to the responding human personality in its social adventures. It is, of course, in *The Build-Up* that we should expect to find the verification of Williams' judgment as to the social chances open to the young Stechers' personalities. Somehow, we can already predict the tendency of their development. They are twentieth-century Americans and the pressures of a middle-class suburban environment will, one suspects, be even harsher with them than was that yeastier provincial milieu which shaped some of the deprived characters of Henry James.

IV

PROSE OTHER THAN FICTION

WILLIAMS' PROSE OTHER THAN FICTION HAS A PARADOXICAL
status in the common estimate of his worth. *In the American Grain*, his brilliant venture in historiography, has ad-
mittedly influenced reassessments of America's past undertaken by other writers in the last two decades. On the
other hand, Williams' enormous output of critical essays,
book reviews, prefaces to other writers' works, editorial
statements, translations, and so on has not had a similar
influence. The scattered and often ephemeral nature of
much of this publication would seem to be one factor
working against his recognition as a provocative and useful critic. Unlike most contemporary poets who have engaged in criticism, Williams has never made a collection
of his critical writing so that his real stature as a critic
is not easily defined. In addition, Williams has somewhat defiantly and sometimes undiplomatically followed a
highly individualistic critical pattern during a period when
criticism in this country, as in England, was least personal

and more "system"-ridden than perhaps at any time in the history of criticism. Unconnected with an academic or institutional setting, and, indeed much opposed to such connections (Williams', like Emerson's, baldly stated and notoriously low opinion of the American university has won him many enemies) his criticism has had to make its own way without authoritarian sanctions, and thus, in the nature of the case, somewhat erratically.

. . . .

In his introduction to the reprint of *In the American Grain* Horace Gregory ably documents the influence of these essays on Hart Crane's *The Bridge*. I think that Archibald MacLeish's *Conquistador* (1932) reveals a similar obligation, especially to the powerful chapters on the destruction of Tenochtitlan, on Cortez, and on De Soto. In addition, Williams' ingenious embedding of authentic source materials in the body of his prose [1] may well have suggested this device in Macleish's narrative poem. I know of at least one major American historian who acknowledges that *In the American Grain* influenced his own researches. But talk of "influence" while interesting is not to my purpose. It is the intention of this still not widely enough read classic which I wish, instead, to consider.

The twenty episodes comprising *In the American Grain* dealing with men and events as separate in time and mean-

[1] Sometimes, in turn, the sources—diaries, chronicles, letters, journals, etc., further color the prose. This is particularly true of the high rhetorical tone of some of the essays and the heavy use of inversion and cadence. The correlation between the source style and Williams' own prose is especially well shown up in "The Discovery of the Indies."

ing as the discovery of the Indies and the discovery of Kentucky, or Edgar Allan Poe and Abraham Lincoln, reveal a common aim. Its nature is quietly defined in a meeting between Williams and Valéry Larbaud.[2] The French man of letters' insight into the American past stimulates the American poet to clarify his own motives: ". . . I speak only of sources. I wish only to disentangle the obscurities that oppress me, to track them to the root and uproot them . . . I seek the support of history but I wish to understand it aright, to make it show itself."

Visibly, then, the task Williams set himself was a tougher one than the mere locating of "usable" pasts. It was to be a more primary exploration and thus a more philosophical one. The question was for Williams not what to *do* with history, but what, in the first place *is* it. What is the American grain? There was no assumption of hortatory responsibility in the investigator. The persuasiveness of the study derives largely from its honesty. Its recovery and discovery of the past are but two aspects of a single quest for understanding. Williams went so far as possible to original sources, to records yet untouched by 'criticism.'

With such a high morality of purpose, it is clear that the scholar of the past cannot slough under the problem of evil in our heritage. There is evil in all men's lives and the American destiny grew out of evil as well as good. The destruction of Tenochtitlan by Cortez is the reverse side of the coin whose other face was Christopher Columbus:

Upon the orchidean beauty of the new world the old rushed inevitably to revenge itself after the Italians' return . . . At the

---

[2] See essay on Père Sebastian Rasles. "Valéry Larbaud" is Paul Valéry.

back . . . it was the evil of the whole world; it was the perennial disappointment which follows like smoke, the bursting of ideas . . .

Columbus is the first victim of America "with its archaic smile." Columbus' tragic story is the story of the degradation of excellence by everything in the world—society, nature, things—which conspires to degrade what is superbly unique. Williams dramatizes this process by presenting Columbus as the cast-out "enemy" of Spain. He turns to Columbus' early diaries whose simple, acute observations, and whose ardent singleness of dedication reveal the good man in all the sharp poetry of his struggle.

What emerges from this study of Columbus and other great men is the tragic paradox of isolation as the cost of greatness. It is this situation which links together figures as remote in temper as De Soto, Raleigh, Champlain, Aaron Burr and Poe. Each of these faced profound conflicts of the spirit, alone. In some instances the physical hardships accompanying the struggle are raised to such a power of negation, as in De Soto's trials, that they tend in themselves to symbolize one aspect of the problem. But whatever the physical terrors, the fact remains that each of these great men was essentially solitary, isolated by his own inner terror of the secret flaws which prey on excellence as well as on mediocrity.

Raleigh's great failure was born of a superb desperation. In the magnificently cadenced introduction to the essay on Raleigh, Williams praises his daring with a formal jubilance, while showing a deep awareness of the tragic undertones:

Of the pursuit of beauty and the husk that remains, perversions and mistakes, while the true form escapes in the wind, sing O Muse:

of Raleigh beloved by majesty, plunging his lust in the body of a new world—and the deaths, misfortunes, counter coups, which swelled back to certify that ardor with defeat. Sing! and let the rumour of these things make the timid more brave and the brave desperate, careless of monuments which celebrate the subtle conversions of sense and let truth go unrecognized . . .

Williams' inspired unsheathing of Raleigh's high and reckless heroism suggests a careful background of knowledge and study. Implicit in Raleigh's defeat is the poverty of our own imaginations which depose excellence if it does not "succeed." But

there is a spirit seeking through America for Raleigh . . . that lost man, seer who failed, planter who never planted, poet whose works are questioned, leader without command, favorite deposed—but one who yet gave title for his Queen, his England, to a coast he never saw but grazed alone with genius.

It is to be expected that not all of Williams' assessments of the past should seem as impervious to temporal readjustments of scale as others. Whether Williams would be willing to stand or fall by his evaluation of the Puritans in 1925 is doubtful. There, if anywhere, he appears to have been affected by the powerful postwar bias which saw the spiritual wasteland of society as unwilled, and inherited from a niggardly, beauty-denying past. Still, this should not suggest that Williams succumbed to the popular rage for historical debunking which characterized the twenties in this country. It was the inner ethics of the Puritan mores that Williams was attacking:

The Pilgrims were mistaken not in what they did, because they went hard to work with their hands and their heads, but in what they imagined for their warmth . . . Everything attests to their

251

despoiled condition . . . So with the low condition of their words
themselves, the bad spelling of their journal . . .

For the wild continent was hostile to a flowering of the
spirit, "forcing it to reproduce its own likeness and no
more."

Rejecting the Puritan stress on "spirit" which he sees as
"an earthly pride which they, prideless, referred to Heaven
and the next world" Williams praises, instead, "Their
tough littleness and weight of many to carry through the
cold." In the twenties, at least, Williams' societal views
appear to have been aristocratic in coloring. Of the Puritans' "talk of commonwealth" he says "common to all alike
so never the proud possession of anyone." The relation of
this heritage to the deficiencies of contemporary America
was bluntly put:

. . . Today it is a generation of gross know-nothingism, of black-
ened churches where hymns groan like chants from stupified jungles,
a generation universally eager to barter permanent values (the hope
of an aristocracy) in return for opportunist material advantages, a
generation hating those whom it obeys.

But a subtler approach to the problem of violence in
America, an approach connected with Williams' definition of the local in art, emerges when he tells Larbaud:

I do believe the average American to be an Indian, but an Indian
robbed of his world unless we call machines a forest in themselves . . . From a lack of touch, lack of belief. Steadily the individual loses caste, then the local government loses its authority; the
head is more and more removed. Finally the center is reached—
totally dehumanized like a Protestant heaven. Everything is Federal-
ized and all laws become prohibitive in essence . . .[3]

---

[3] See essay on Père Sebastian Rasles.

He is critical of the tendency of American historians to see the time too near and to succumb to a parochialism characterized by a "universal lack of scale." Writing on Thomas Morton, he says:

. . . It is not so much good history to present Morton with sly amusement in mortal and unmannerly conduct with his betters, as it would be to relieve him from that imposition of his time and seriously to show up that lightness, his essential character, which disclosed the Puritans themselves as maimed, to their advantage, for their survival . . .

It is this "essential character" which emerges in the study of Benjamin Franklin ("he's sort of proud of his commonness, isn't he?") and which in the essay on Aaron Burr ironically titled "The Virtue of History" impels Williams to "smash the shell of history" and see the man inside, for ". . . history follows governments and never men."

Like Eliot in England, like Ransom and others in this country, in short like a generation or two of critical opinion running counter to the powerful currents of Marxian determinism, what Williams argued was to see the past as a series of discrete particulars, rather than as a detemporized abstraction. It is clear, of course, that either theory of history sacrifices part of the picture for the sake of the frame. Williams saves himself from the limitations of his frame by his keen sense of event or "environment" as it interacts with personality. That is to say, his concept of personality is sufficiently plastic to admit exterior circumstance as part of its structure. In this way it is possible for him to find men entirely great as *men*, rather than as mere incarnations of abstract forces, while, at the same time,

253

grounding their uniqueness in a place, a time, and an action.

This comes out with keen beauty in the slightly old-fashioned narrative of the Daniel Boone essay. Boone, to Williams, had seen the problem of the new world as a moral and an aesthetic one: "to bathe in, to explore, always more deeply, to see, to feel, to touch . . . If the land was to be possessed it must be as the Indian possessed it." It was not for Boone to be an Indian, but the reverse "to be *himself* in a new world, Indian-like."

It is precisely such self-affirmation through self-surrender which Williams is unable to credit to America's pioneers and statesmen. In another essay he writes of the Puritans: "The character they had . . . was that of giving their fine energy, as they must have done, to the smaller, narrower, protective thing and not to the great New World." Yet along with the plaintive sense of loss, there goes the compassionate recognition of the human dilemma. How can men be better than themselves? How can they outreach the conditions of their small humanness?

It is because of his recognition of the varied potentials of the human spirit that Williams is able to see Aaron Burr in the plausible, even winning image of a man doomed to failure by the very excess of his gifts, an excess which manifested itself by a talent for nonconformity. The popular and indeed the official view of Burr as a dissolute Machiavellian, cunning and ambitious, gives way to that of an imprudent, impulsive man and an over-sensitive aesthete. "He was a bad scholar of his betters—whose schemes succeeded." The background of personal animosity between Washington and Burr is not sloughed under in favor of the President. Williams is capable of an artistic detachment which can enthrone Washington as hero in one work [4] and in another expose his limitations when opposed to someone like Burr: "Burr knew what democracy must liberate . . . Men intact with all their senses working . . . If politics could be the science of humanity, I think his place was there."

Williams' view of democracy, obviously, is one of a philosophical purity. The liberation of the individual, rather than the glorification of the masses, is the recurring and insistent emphasis of the essays. It is this that makes it possible for Williams to understand Burr's resentment of the levelling influence of the new government, and in the same volume to write a prose-ballad celebrating the anonymous Negro whose unique quality makes a special contribution to the life about us.[5] The flexibility of Williams' approach to American experience in such diverse pieces shows him to be operating in the best tradition of the personal essay. One tends to forget that it is personality which makes the personal essay.

Remembering this, the volatility of Williams' shifts from socio-political to socio-aesthetic appraisals seems not only just but inevitable. For Williams' aesthetic is closely grounded in his view of society, as his critical vocabulary suggests. The metaphorical cast of an artist's thought will tell more about relationships than a bibliography of sources. So, for example, the social valuation put upon being an Indian in a new world (seen as a lost chance

[4] See the discussion of the *George Washington Libretto* under THE PLAYS.
[5] See "The Advent of the Slaves."

255

for Americans) crops up in Williams' graceful and heretical essay on Poe.

In it Williams' militant defense of American letters is carefully geared to Poe's own distinction between "nationality" which the latter slights, and the function of the local, of place, which he emphasizes as necessary to imaginative action:

With Poe, words were not hung by usage with associations, the pleasing wraith of former masteries . . . With Poe words were figures; an old language truly, but one from which he carried over only the most elemental qualities to his new purpose, which was to find a way to tell his soul . . . He sought by stress upon construction to hold the loose-strung mass off even at the cost of an icy coldness of appearance; it was the first need of his time, an escape from the formless mass he hated. It is the very sense of a beginning, as is the impulse which drove him to the character of all his tales; to get from sentiment to form, a backstroke from the swarming "population."

Shrewdly, Williams points out that Poe's lonely efforts to annihilate the false drove him underground so that "he emerges as ghoulish." The French have been "attracted by the surface of his genius and copy the wrong thing . . . the strange, the bizarre (the recoil) without sensing the actuality of which that is the compliment . . ." Poe abhorred the opportune, counseling American writers against writing of Indians, forests, or natural beauties. "His whole insistence has been upon method, in opposition to nameless rapture over nature . . . He counsels writers to *borrow nothing* from the scene, but to put all the weight of the effort into the writing."

Williams does not make the mistake of overestimating Poe's achievement. Poe was great for his "conception of

256

a *possibility.*" His recoil was equally against a facile imitativeness of English modes as it was against a vulgar parochialism. Poe hoped "to originate a style that does spring from local condition, not of trees and mountains but of the soul." He fell into difficulties because in America the soul was starved. "He is known as a poet, yet there are but five poems, possibly three." The least mystery of his work are the poems, which are himself, "the accumulation of all that he has expressed, in the criticism, in the prose tales . . ." In the poems the full force of Poe's isolation comes down upon him. "His passion for the refrain is like an echo from a hollow. It is his own voice returning—" In this probing study of Poe the crude and misstated notions held about Williams' own "localism" receive their most eloquent refutation. Williams' idea of the local, of place, and of art as place raised to the universal, is easier to examine impartially when explored in the context of another writer's performance. The essay on Poe is a superb exploration of Williams' own aesthetic along with that of Poe.

In the American Grain closes with a brief appreciation of Lincoln. The daring image by which Williams isolates Lincoln's quality of brooding tenderness toward his people and his trust is typical of his method: ". . . a woman in an old shawl—with a great bearded face . . . holding all fearfully together." To Williams, Lincoln is a symbol of the failures and the possibilities implicit in the American grain. In the closing passage of this unorthodox appraisal Williams reaffirms his perception of the delicate, mercurial line, the utterly ambivalent pattern by which the American grain can be discerned. For in Lincoln's tragic experience "is reflected the brutalizing desolation of life in America up to that time; yet perversely flowering." The Civil War is seen to punctuate the end of an era: "It was the end of THAT PERIOD." There is a warning as well as a hope implied.

. . . .

A valuable aspect of Williams' activity in prose fields is his translation of work from the French and the Spanish. His childhood bilingualism (English and Spanish) as well as his brief adolescent schooling in Switzerland and France have no doubt contributed to the colloquial grace of his renderings. His best-known translation is that of Philippe Soupault's *Last Nights of Paris*. Soupault, a poet, whom Matthew Josephson identifies as the "spiritual heir of Guillaume Apollinaire . . . the most authentic of Dadaists," seems to a contemporary reader to bear a considerable resemblance to the Existentialists. I imagine Williams was attracted to this deft little novel of Parisian low life by its fresh and simple acceptance of the poetry and "the great mystery of common diurnal things." The task was initially undertaken to amuse Williams' aged mother who was going blind. She was his co-translator.

But whether it was the clear and beautiful texture of Soupault's prose or the theme which was most congenial, the result is a lucid and persuasive translation. The operations of chance and fate which provide the only formal "plot" for *Last Nights of Paris* suggests that it is (as indeed do other elements in Dada) a forerunner of literary Existentialism. In Soupault's novel the "I" hero is drawn into the accidents of the night, just as is the hero of Camus'

The Stranger (written twenty years later), through a kind of torpor. Like the involuntary murderer of Camus' novel, he participates quite innocently in certain conspiratorial activities which never become clearly defined. Even the dramatis personae are remarkably alike. Both books, born of two great wars, reveal how deeply the fiber of despair is twined into the French psyche.

As in *The Stranger* the swift and economical events involve a quest for certitude, on *any* terms; that is to say, a quest for positive action, even if anti-social. Eventually, chance is itself paradoxically established as the only certainty. Georgette, the birdlike prostitute and her mysterious assignations eventually become a city in themselves. The "labyrinthine ways" of the city of night is, in essence, the story.

As Pound and Eliot are so fond of arguing, the discipline of the worker with language is served by exposure to other languages, and, in particular, by the gymnastic limbering-up to be got in translating styles remote from his own temperamental verbal bias. The objectivity of Williams' Flaubertian prose in his own fiction is almost a polar opposite to Soupault's metaphorical subjectivism.

The range of Williams' linguistic appreciations are demonstrated by other translations, but all in common suggest that it is the texture of the writing which is his first criterion of interest. Among various translations from the Spanish, *The Man Who Resembled a Horse* from the Guatemalan poet and novelist, Rafael Martínez, is the only published one.[6] Williams acknowledges as his collaborator "My father who really did the work on the trans-

[6] *New Directions Annual No. 8.*

lation of this story . . ." Martínez is described as "The creator of an original and interesting type of short story known as the psycho-zoological tale." *The Man Who Resembled a Horse* is a moral fable with Freudian and sociological nuances welded into a surrealist design. The extraordinary Señor de Aretal first captivates the narrator by godlike qualities of crystalline brilliance and then gradually reveals himself in the aspect of a horse as he takes on the hues of his inferior companions. Eventually, a crucial choice is forced on the narrator:

Which is the true spirit of Señor de Aretal? And I answered it quickly. Señor de Aretal with his fine mentality had no soul: he was amoral. He was amoral as a horse and allowed himself to be mounted by any spirit whatever . . . That moral vacuum of his being would fill, as do all vacuums, with ease. It tended to fill itself.

Obviously this is a critical parable of the artist. Still, the moral is more oblique than this brief quotation suggests. A dualism in man is posited. But it is more subtle than the conventional body-soul dualism. Man is not merely animal and spiritual, but rather crystalline-fiery and dense-solid. The brute nobility of the animal is admired for its brutishness. Love is the power which heals the split in man's double nature. Señor de Aretal is not just a man who resembled a horse, but all men, all of whom resemble horses. The allegorical climate of this brilliant piece is foreign to Williams' own temper, but Martínez' emphasis on love as redemption is like that which signs all of Williams' later work with a seal of affirmation.

Among other translations from the Spanish are the play *My Excellency,* an amusing social satire from the contemporary Spanish of Luis Rechani Agrait,[7] and *The Dog and The Fever*,[8] a sixteenth-century Gongorist *novela* by Don Francesco de Quevedo. As these translations indicate, Williams' curiosity is not limited by his own creative commitments. The considerable gift which he has brought to the exacting discipline of making foreign works available to an English-reading audience deserves wider recognition than it has yet received.

. . . .

It is apart from my purpose to give a chronological account of Williams' critical activities. I hope that my discussion of Williams' writing has made it clear that his basic attitudes toward the problems of art, or, rather, toward the critical formulation of these problems has been fairly consistent. I have attempted wherever feasible to work out my exposition of a particular context through the selective use of Williams' own critical and aesthetic statements. However, since some of this material may be overlooked in the occasional inattentiveness to footnotes and quotations which one may expect from even the friendliest reader, I shall recapitulate Williams' general critical position.

Williams might, I think, be usefully described as a Deweyan instrumentalist in his approach to art.[9] This

[7] U.B. Collection. Act III is missing or was not completed.

[8] MS IV. The translation was made in collaboration with Williams' mother.

[9] Williams in conversation has often expressed his appreciation of *Art as Experience*. This, of course, does not prove a direct influence. Most of Williams' critical values were formulated before the publication of Dewey's work in aesthetics in 1934.

comment, however, requires further exposition. In *Art as Experience* Dewey writes:

> The problem of the relation of art and morals is too often treated as if the problem existed only on the side of art. It is virtually assumed that morals are satisfactory in idea if not in fact, and that the only question is whether and in what ways art should conform to a moral system already developed . . . Were art an acknowledged power in human association . . . and were morals understood to be identical with every aspect of value that is shared in experience, the "problem" of the relationship between art and morals would not exist . . . Because art is wholly innocent of ideas derived from praise and blame, it is looked upon with the eye of suspicion by the guardians of custom, or only the art that is itself so old and "classic" as to receive conventional praise is grudgingly admitted . . . Yet this indifference to praise and blame because of preoccupation with imaginative experience constitutes the heart of the moral potency of art . . . The first intimations of wide and large reductions of purpose are of necessity imaginative . . .[10]

Williams' familiar insistence on the "new," often mistaken for mere novelty is, in reality, an insistence on the uncodified and the fresh in experience as a means of liberating potentiality for greater vision. It is strikingly similar to Dewey's analysis of the conventional association of Art and Morality. Williams' emphasis on "contact" (touch), a principle reminiscent of E. M. Forster's battle-cry, "Only connect!" and on the "local" is a technique for achieving such regeneration in art. His long-familiar and often derided advice to the artist to go to the life about him and especially to the living vulgar language of daily life for the nourishment of the imagination finds confirmation in Dewey:

[10] Pp. 387 ff.

PROSE OTHER THAN FICTION

All the "fine" arts in order not to become merely refined have to be renewed from time to time by closer contact with materials outside the aesthetic tradition. But literature in particular is the one most in need of constant refreshment from this source, since it has at command material already eloquent, pregnant, picturesque and general in its appeal, and yet most subject to convention and stereotype . . . language is informed with the temperament and the ways of viewing and interpreting life that are characteristic of the culture of a continuing social group . . . The architectural, pictorial and sculptural are always unconsciously surrounded and enriched by values that proceed from speech . . . The imaginative force of literature is in the intensification of the idealizing office performed by words in ordinary speech . . . (In literary art) words as media are not exhausted in their power to convey possibility.[11]

Williams has publicly acknowledged his acceptance of Dewey's conclusions, conclusions, as has been pointed out, quite congenial to his own:

John Dewey has given us the lead. He says: We are beginning to discover that the local is the universal. That is to say we are to discover the universals of poetry in our own language and until we do so we shall not have a poetry of our own.[12]

In another characteristic passage written considerably before the appearance of Dewey's analysis, Williams had written:

"It is impossible to remake the country." Quite so, but it is not impossible to remake the country in the *imagination* . . . That which is living is that which concerns me. I want to place a value on everything I touch and I want to place the human elements first . . . There is nothing in just revolt . . . So the revolt I plan is in my place, in America, to throw out the unrealizable elements

---

[11] *Ibid.*, pp. 240 ff.

[12] From notes for an article, "A Few General Correctives to the Present State of American Poetry" for the *Columbia College Literary Journal.* (MS V).

of my construction and make it of the unused stuff of my history and my present, to get rid of everything that I do not know . . . *In my place*—isn't that the way the profoundest ethical revolutions have *begun?*

Williams, like Dewey, had rejected the familiar opposition of art and morality and he, too, made the same confident identification of an imaginative with an ethical revolution. But to revitalize a culture implies, as Williams recognizes, not brute revolt, but rather a plastic exercise of the historical sense. For Williams, as for Dewey:

There is no art in which there is only a single tradition. The critic who is not intimately aware of a variety of traditions is of necessity limited and his criticisms will be one-sided to the point of distortion . . .

This knowledge of many traditions is no foe to discrimination . . . Knowledge of a wide range of traditions is a condition of exact and severe discrimination. For only by means of such a knowledge can the critic detect the intent of an artist and the adequacy of his execution of intent . . .[13]

In an essay *Constancy and Freedom,* written in his early twenties, Williams, following his then formal Emersonian practice of polarizing abstractions (other essays of this period are *Waste and Use, Faith and Knowledge,* etc.) considers a similar problem. We seek two opposites, "Liberty . . . the motion, and constancy the no-motion . . . change against the unchanged; the new against the old and the permanent . . ." Examining the seeming antithesis further, he finds of liberty that "The first property is that it is comparative . . . Thus we have the spectacle of freedom yearning after constancy or permanence in order to be freer . . ." Tradition, then, is seen not as ir-

[13] *Art as Experience,* pp. 313–314.

revocably poised, Gibraltar-like, against invention but rather as having a parallel growth with it. Each major invention effects an alteration in the character of tradition. It is the recognition of this kind of dynamic—tradition energizing invention, invention, in turn, revitalizing tradition—which animates all of Williams' best work.

How all the facets of Williams' aesthetic merge into a single stream of discovery is, of course, best illustrated by his non-critical writing. Briefly put, his grounding is a pragmatic one: to know the only world we can know, sharply and fully with all our senses, to formulate intellectual patterns from this perception of brute particulars, configurations which, in turn, becoming too abstract must be replenished from a new exploration of the concrete. "To raise what is under our noses to the imagination," to create the universal from the local, to fecundate tradition with new experience, this is the radical "primitivism" which Williams' narrower critics decry. In reality, Williams has at no time been the victim of Rousseauian self-indulgence. In an unpublished essay, written more than thirty years ago, he says:

There is but one thing we can know directly and that is the world we own and we do own it, which is not so insignificant a matter after all . . . I can only look with surprise on those who bewail their own lost innocence. . . . The innocence of a child is good but . . . the innocence of a man is nobler.

John Dewey, writing about a similar relationship many years later in *Art as Experience* ranks literature as the highest of the arts because language particularizes "the generality of potentiality." And he concludes: "For all we know of any situation is what it does to and with us:

that is *its* nature." It is not extravagant to say that Williams throughout all his difficult and passionate explorations has sought precisely that: to know of his situation what it does to and with him and thus, in the end, to discover *its* nature, and so, perhaps, his own.

BIBLIOGRAPHY

THE SCATTERED NATURE OF MUCH OF WILLIAMS' PUBLICATION
during some forty years makes a complete bibliography a
subject for a study in itself. All the collected writings and
important single pieces published in anthologies and magazines are listed here. Secondary studies present no bibliographical problem. There are regrettably few of any
critical merit. There are innumerable newspaper and
magazine reviews of which I have mentioned only a few
since, for the most part, they add little to the reader's
understanding. The Lockwood Memorial Library of the
University of Buffalo has a Williams MS Collection which
I have utilized extensively. The collection includes several
thousand items and is as yet unindexed. Except in a few
instances, publication outlets are not indicated. The collection provides a mine of source material for the critic,
as well as the bibliographer and biographer, for it includes
many work sheets and early drafts. A full bibliographical
record of Williams' publication in the many short-lived

267

and now increasingly rare little magazines to which he has contributed is much needed.

I. WILLIAM CARLOS WILLIAMS

1. Books

Poems, pamphlet privately printed by Reid Howell, Rutherford (New Jersey), 1909.

The Tempers, Elkin Matthews, London, 1913.

Kora in Hell: Improvisations, The Four Seas Company, Boston, 1917.

Al Que Quiere!, The Four Seas Company, Boston, 1920. The exclamation point of the title is omitted in the *CCP* which adds a parenthetical Englishing, thus: "(To Him Who Wants It)."

Sour Grapes, The Four Seas Company, Boston, 1921.

Spring and All, Contact Publishing Company, 1922, 1923 (?).

The Great American Novel, The Three Mountains Press, Paris, 1923.

In the American Grain, Albert and Charles Boni, New York, 1925. (Reprinted by New Directions, Norfolk, Connecticut, 1939, with an introduction by Horace Gregory.

A Voyage to Pagany, The Macaulay Company, New York, 1928.

A Novelette and Other Prose, Imprimerie F. Cabasson, Toulon, France, 1932.

The Knife of the Times, The Dragon Press, Ithaca (New York), 1932.

The Cod Head, Contempo, Chapel Hill, 1932. Also Harvest Press, San Francisco, 1932. Pamphlet.

Collected Poems, 1921–1931, Objectivist Press, New York, 1934. With a preface by Wallace Stevens.

An Early Martyr, The Alcestis Press, New York, 1935.

Adam & Eve and The City, The Alcestis Press, New York, 1936.

White Mule, New Directions, Norfolk (Connecticut), 1937.

The Complete Collected Poems of William Carlos Williams, New Directions, Norfolk (Connecticut), 1938.

In the Money, New Directions, Norfolk (Connecticut), 1940.

First Act, New Directions, Norfolk (Connecticut), 1946. (Reprint of *White Mule* and *In the Money* in one-volume edition).

BIBLIOGRAPHY

The Broken Span, pamphlet in *The Poet of the Month Series,* New Directions, Norfolk (Connecticut), 1941.

The Wedge, The Cummington Press, Cummington (Massachusetts), 1944.

Paterson, Book I, New Directions, New York, 1946.

Paterson, Book II, New Directions, New York, 1948.

A Dream of Love, Direction 6, New Directions, New York, 1948.

The Clouds, The Wells College Press and The Cummington Press, 1948.

The Pink Church, Golden Goose Press, Columbus (Ohio), 1949.

2. Translations

Last Nights of Paris, from the French of Philippe Soupault, The Macaulay Company, New York, 1929.

"The Man Who Resembled a Horse" from the Spanish of Rafael Martínez in *New Directions Annual No. 8,* Norfolk (Connecticut), 1944.

3. Uncollected Pieces

Contact, New York, December 1920–June 1923. Five issues. A magazine edited with Robert McAlmon. Includes many Williams items.

Mannikin, Williams Issue, No. 2, New York, 1923. Edited by Monroe Wheeler. Contains several poems not included in *CCP.*

Contact (new series), February 1932. Three issues. Edited with Nathaniel West. Contains many Williams items.

"The First President, Libretto for an Opera on George Washington," in *The New Caravan,* edited by Kreymborg, Mumford and Rosenfeld. W. W. Norton and Company, New York, 1936.

"From: A Folded Skyscraper," in *The American Caravan* edited by Brooks, Kreymborg, Mumford and Rosenfeld. Macaulay Company, New York, 1927. Two prose sketches have never been reprinted.

"The Atlantic City Convention," in *The Second American Caravan* edited by Kreymborg, Mumford, and Rosenfeld. The Macaulay

Company, New York, 1928. A prose "speech" accompanying the poem has never been reprinted.

"A Point for American Criticism" in *Our Exagmination round his Factification for Incamination* by Samuel Beckett, Frank Budgen, Stuart Gilbert and others. Shakespeare and Company, Paris, 1929. (Reprinted as An *Exagmination of James Joyce*, New Directions, Norfolk (Connecticut), 1939.

Active Anthology, edited by Ezra Pound. Faber and Faber, London, 1933. Includes some poems not reprinted in the *CCP*.

"The Thirty Cantos of Ezra Pound," in *The Rocking Horse*, Spring, 1935 (publication of the Arden Club, University of Wisconsin).

"The Work of Gertrude Stein," in *Pagany*, Winter, 1930.

"The Invisible University" in *Trend* (University of Chicago), No. 1, 1942.

"Four Stories" in *New Directions Annual No. 3*, Norfolk (Connecticut), 1939.

"Retorting," in *Retort* I, 56, Spring, 1943.

"Comedy Entombed" in *New Directions Annual No. 9*, Norfolk (Connecticut), 1946.

William Carlos Williams, Issue No. 11 of *Briarcliff Quarterly*, Briarcliff Manor (New York), October 1946.

Edited by Norman Macleod and Vivienne Koch. Contains poems, photographs of Williams, Chapter I of *The Build-Up* and critical studies of his work, etc. For critical articles see Secondary Studies.

"An Approach to the Poem" in *English Institute Studies*, Columbia University Press, New York, 1948. A paper read at the meeting of the Institute in 1947.

II. SECONDARY STUDIES

No complete book has been written about Williams. The following references contain chapters or sections dealing with him or his work.

Aiken, Conrad. *Scepticisms: Notes on Contemporary Poetry*, 1919.

Early impressionistic 'appreciation' of the poetry.

BIBLIOGRAPHY

Aldington, Richard. *Life for Life's Sake,*
Useful for historical and biographical data on Williams' connection with the Imagists. Uncritical.

Anderson, Margaret. *My Thirty Years' War,* Covici, Friede, New York, 1930.
Personalia and gossip of the middle years. Useful bibliographic material.

Blackmur, R. P. *The Expense of Greatness,* Arrow Editions, New York, 1930.
A brief critique of the *Complete Collected Poems* on their publication in 1939.

Hoffman, Allen, and Ulrich. *The Little Magazine,* Princeton University Press, Princeton (New Jersey), 1946.
Williams is treated as a key figure in the history of the little magazine. Important for its excellent bibliographic data on Williams' numerous connections with little magazines.

McAlmon, Robert. *Being Geniuses Together,* Secker and Warburg, London, 1938.
Anecdotal. May be of use to future biographers.

Monroe, Harriet. *A Poet's Life,* The Macmillan Company, New York, 1938.
Interesting source materials (letters, etc.) and editorial impressions of Williams.

Pound, Ezra. *Pavannes and Divisions,* A. A. Knopf, New York, 1919.
See "A Retrospect" for source material on Imagism.

———— *Polite Essays,* New Directions, Norfolk (Connecticut), n.d.
See "Dr. Williams' Position," reprinted from *The Dial,* November 1928. A perceptive but somewhat rambling study chiefly concerned with *A Voyage to Pagany.*

Rosenfeld, Paul. *Port of New York,* Harcourt, Brace and Company, New York, 1924.
A thoughtful early appraisal of the poetry.

Shapiro, Karl. "The Meaning of the Discarded Poem" in *Poets at Work*" by Arnheim, Auden, Shapiro and Stauffer, Harcourt, Brace and Company, New York, 1948.
A brief and disappointing study of the work sheets of an unpublished Williams' poem.

Taupin, René. *L'Influence du Symbolisme Français sur La Poésie Américaine,* H. Champion, Paris, 1929.

> A serious critical study of Williams' poetic achievement in the first two decades of his career in which he is seen as Gallic in spirit and as the heir of the Symbolists.

Winters, Yvor. *Primitivism and Decadence,* Arrow Editions, New York, 1937.

> A brilliant if ambivalent study of Williams' verse in which the writer oscillates between admiration for Williams as an "experimentalist" with a rich traditional residue, and his fear of Williams' "primitivism." The thesis sometimes dulls the individual perception.

2. Articles and Reviews

Burke, Kenneth. "Heaven's First Law" *The Dial,* February 22, 1922.

> An enthusiastic review of *Sour Grapes.*

"The Methods of William Carlos Williams," *The Dial,* February 1927.

> A provocative study as revealing of Burke as of Williams.

Deutsch, Babette. "The Complete Collected Poems," *The Nation,* November 19, 1938.

> An urbane retrospective evaluation.

Jarrell, Randall. "The Poet and His Public," *Partisan Review,* September–October 1946.

> A useful paraphrase of *Paterson, Book I.*

Lowell, Robert. "Paterson II," *The Nation,* June 19, 1948.

> An appreciative and convincing exegesis of *Paterson, Book II.*

Moore, Marianne. "Things Others Never Notice," *Poetry* (Chicago), May 1934.

> The title is the theme of this appreciation.

Morgan, Frederick. "William Carlos Williams: Imagery, Rhythm, Form," *The Sewanee Review,* October–December 1947.

> A serious but narrowly conceived study of Williams as an "Imagist."

Rakosi, Carl. "William Carlos Williams," *The Symposium,* October 1933.

> Judgment by a fellow Objectivist.

272

BIBLIOGRAPHY

Stearns, Marshall W. "Syntax, Sense and Sound in Dr. Williams,"
    Poetry (Chicago), April 1945.
    An illustration of the persistent critical reliance on Wallace
    Stevens' early judgment of Williams as "anti-poetic."
Stevens, Wallace; Tyler, Parker; Moore, Marianne and others. *William Carlos Williams*, Issue No. 6, *Briarcliff Quarterly*, October
    1946.
    Critical studies and brief tributes. The essay by Parker Tyler on
    Paterson, Book I is the best analysis of it yet made.
Zukofsky, Louis. "American Poetry 1920–30," *The Symposium*,
    January 1931.
    Astute early study which emphasizes Williams' roots in the
    tradition of English poetry.

INDEX

274

INDEX

INDEX

277